TAKE THE SLOW ROAD
# ENGLAND
# & WALES

For Lizzy.
And for everyone else who knows that if it's
worth having, it can be bought with a smile.

CONWAY
Bloomsbury Publishing Plc
50 Bedford Square, London, WC1B 3DP, UK

BLOOMSBURY, CONWAY and the Conway logo
are trademarks of Bloomsbury Publishing Plc

First published in Great Britain 2019

publisher regret any inconvenience caused if
addresses have changed or sites have ceased to exist,
but can accept no responsibility for any such changes.

A catalogue record for this book is available from
the British Library

Library of Congress Cataloguing-in-Publication data
has been applied for

ISBN:    PB: 978-1-84486-535-2
         ePub: 978-1-84486-534-5
         ePDF: 978-1-84486-536-9

10  9  8  7  6  5  4

Designed and typeset by Austin Taylor
Typeset in Catamaran, Janda and Raleway

Printed and bound in Italy
by Printer Trento s.r.l.

Bloomsbury Publishing Plc makes every effort to
ensure that the papers used in the manufacture
of our books are natural, recyclable products
made from wood grown in well-managed forests.
Our manufacturing processes conform to the
environmental regulations of the country of origin.

To find out more about our authors and books visit
www.bloomsbury.com and sign up for our newsletters

# TAKE THE SLOW ROAD

# ENGLAND & WALES

Inspirational Journeys Round England and Wales
by Camper Van and Motorhome

## MARTIN DOREY

C☒NWAY

LONDON · OXFORD · NEW YORK · NEW DELHI · SYDNEY

# CONTENTS

About this book 7
How to use this book 8
Introducing England 10
Introducing Wales 12
How to get to England
  and Wales 14
What to take with you 16
Eating on your travels 21
Where and how to stay
  in England and Wales 24

## THE SOUTH WEST 30

01 ST IVES TO SENNEN 33
02 EXETER TO PORTLAND BILL 45
03 THE EXMOOR COAST 55
04 THE ATLANTIC HIGHWAY 65
05 BODMIN MOOR 75
06 BRISTOL TO YEOVIL 85
07 THE RIVER DART 97

## THE SOUTH AND SOUTH EAST 108

08 SOUTH COAST SPRAWL 111
09 DARTFORD TO ABINGDON 121
10 SALISBURY TO UCKFIELD 135

## EAST ANGLIA 148

11 BEYOND SOUTHWOLD 151
12 NORTH NORFOLK 163

## THE MIDLANDS 172

13 THE WHITE PEAK 175
14 DERWENT AND THE
   DARK PEAK 185

## WALES 194

15 WALES COAST TO COAST 197
16 WEST WALES 215
17 THE PEMBROKESHIRE
   COAST NATIONAL PARK 225

## THE NORTH WEST 238

18 KESWICK AND BORROWDALE 241
19 KIRKSTONE PASS 249
20 WINDERMERE AND CONISTON 257

## THE NORTH 266

21 HARROGATE AND WHARFEDALE 269
22 HEXHAM TO BARNARD CASTLE 279
23 GATESHEAD TO GREENHEAD
   VIA HADRIAN'S WALL 289

## THE NORTH EAST 296

24 YORK AND NORTH YORKSHIRE 299
25 SALTBURN TO SCARBOROUGH 309
26 FROM TEESSIDE TO TYNESIDE 319
27 TYNEMOUTH TO BAMBURGH 329
28 BAMBURGH TO ROCHESTER 339

CAMPER VAN AND MOTORHOME HIRE 346   INDEX 350

# ABOUT THIS BOOK

Hello.
Welcome.
Or welcome back, to the slow road.

If you've already taken the slow road to Scotland in the first book in this series, then you'll already know what it's all about. But if you are new to this meandering, slothful way of travelling, then I hope – I know – you'll love it.

Taking the slow road means taking time to enjoy the journey, whether you're in a motorhome or a camper van, or even if you're touring in the car. It means stopping to pop the kettle on and getting out to stretch your legs somewhere really, really brilliant. It's about exploring with time on your side, touring gently, moving slowly, and savouring as much as you can of our lovely country.

And it is lovely.

It has peaks, dales, rivers, beaches, highways and byways, single tracks and high mountain passes.

With a turn of the key you can explore them all.

So stop reading and get in the van.

See you on the road.

# HOW TO USE THIS BOOK

**Honestly, it's not rocket science** using this book.
But it may be useful to know why it's been written the way
it has. As you flick through the pages you'll see that there
are a number of routes. These are my suggestions for great
roads and routes to explore, for whatever reason. Some are
great for wild swimming, some for walking, some for cycling.
Others are just good for the landscapes they take you
through or the sites they join up.

Each route is separated into two sections. The first is the story of when
I was there and what meant most for me about the route. In North Devon
and North Cornwall, where I live, the route is all about exploring out-of-
the-way beaches, simply because there are so many of them. They are a

feature of the geography of that most lovely corner of England. So it stands to reason that I'd want to talk about what it means to me to be there. It's also the bit that I hope will inspire you to get in the van or motorhome and go. Those experiences can be yours too.

The second part of each route is the practical stuff, the 'how to'. This is important as it's designed to help you follow the route. Of course, you don't have to follow it to the letter – and I'd love it if you didn't – but it will at least give you an idea of what to expect along the way. Use it in your planning to make a trip for yourself. Maps will help you do this too, as will the information bits at the end of each chapter. There are ideas of things to do and see as well as places to stay. These are my selections and they are largely based on my experience. If a campsite you love isn't in the book, it probably means I haven't been there so can't comment.

Finally, if you don't have a van, there are details of local hire companies where you can rent a vehicle for yourself to have that adventure of a lifetime (that you'll probably want to do again and again and again). Renting a van is the perfect way to find out if living that kind of a life is for you.

I hope it will be.

# INTRODUCING ENGLAND

It's a funny little country, this England.

It's busy, a little clogged up in places, and often eccentric. It has bonkers politics and notions of grandeur, a crazy, unchecked press and a terrible sense of entitlement that's a hangover from colonial giddiness. England has divisions between north and south, rich and poor and the very, very rich and the 'just a little bit middle England who'd rather be cast asunder than kowtow to Johnny Foreigner' class. England is full of castles, some terraced, some on private estates, and some on promontories overlooking the sea.

It's a funny little place.

But hold it right there. Let's forget about the history, the politics and the social divisions and look at England as a piece of land for exploring. Let's look at it as a place. That's what we're here for.

England is the country of my birth. It is the place I have spent most of my life, as a child riding a bike through the Chiltern Hills, as a student navigating the streets of Manchester, as a young trier learning his way around the London Underground, as a dropout exploring the coasts of Devon and Cornwall with a late-in-life partner, and, finally, as a dad looking to introduce his kids to a wholesome way of life on the ocean.

Hitting the road for this book made me realise that England isn't just about towns, cities, motorways and junctions, although it has a lot of them. Between the conurbations and built-up areas England has some very fine scenery, some brilliant camping and some absolutely brilliant driving. It has around 6,000 miles of coastline (depending on how you measure it), ten National Parks, more than 40 Areas of Outstanding Natural Beauty, almost 400 lakes bigger than 2.5 acres and a couple of half-decent mountains, if you like them diddly.

England has fens and levels, hills, peaks, dales, scarps, edges, combes, moors, burrows, chases and even a few downs. It has islands that aren't islands and islands that are sometimes islands and sometimes not. It has woods and forests, glades and dingly dells.

And I love it. Simply because it's beautiful.

Choosing where to go for this book was really tricky. I wanted to cover as much of the country as possible during the year it took me to write it, but there are just so many roads to choose from so I am pretty sure I've missed some real corkers! Even so, there are some good 'uns in here.

England's road network consists of around 188,500 miles of road, including motorways and urban and rural A, B and C roads. The vast majority of our roads are classed as minor roads (over 80% of the total), with rural minor roads being the largest single type.

There's a lot of tarmac out there.

England has 76.5% of all the roads in Great Britain, which is surprising as it accounts for only just over half the total area. I guess that proves it's a busy little place. Motorways, which account for just 2,300 miles of the UK's overall network (that's about 1%), take 21% of the traffic. The A roads take a further 44.4% of the traffic, which leaves just 34.6% of the traffic enjoying 87.3% of the road length.

If you ever wanted a reason to avoid the motorways and take the slow road, this is it.

Put the old girl in gear and find your pocket of paradise.

# INTRODUCING WALES

Wales is small, but it's never ignored. You might say that this proud little country, the thorn in the side of England, is punching well above its weight. It has been used many times over as a rough unit of comparative measurement, which implies that we can all imagine how big it actually is – which is around 21,000 square kilometres, in case you were wondering.

Wales has it all, even though it may not have as many words for everything as we have in England. It has five peaks over 1,000m, including Snowdon (England's highest, Scafell Pike, is only 978m), its own set of Seven

Wonders, a spectacular cave system, hundreds of miles of fantastic beaches, high passes, long, elegant rivers, a tiny city, three National Parks and five Areas of Outstanding Natural Beauty.

I love Wales, and I always have, ever since I first camped there as a child. Later, in my student days, I spent a lot of time driving to North Wales to camp and surf. It was travelling up the west coast for *Coast* magazine that gave me the idea of writing *Take the Slow Road* in the first place. And that article was inspired by a trip circumnavigating the country for my second book, *The Camper Van Coast*. Now that my mum lives in Ireland I get to dawdle through Wales regularly on my way to Holyhead or Pembroke Dock. It's always a pleasure.

In short, I have been enjoying a love affair with Wales for a long time now. So exploring it a little more was never going to be a chore. Wales, to me, means climbing Snowdon, jumping into the Blue Lagoon, exploring the Wye Valley, driving over the Brecon Beacons, coasteering in St David's.

In terms of roads, Wales is still quite little. With just 8% of the UK road network, it sometimes lacks choice, due to the terrain. That means there are more A roads there than in England. But that doesn't really matter. Like Scotland, Wales's roads are a delight, even if they are 'major' routes. The A479, which bisects the country, is an absolute cracker, while even the A5, the main route to Holyhead, has some incredible moments when it reaches Snowdonia.

That means you can put a pin in the map and almost guarantee a win. Which makes it perfect for a slow road adventure.

# HOW TO GET TO ENGLAND AND WALES

**Humour me here, please?** Thank you.

England and Wales are countries that make up part of the United Kingdom of Great Britain and Northern Ireland. They sit in the main land mass of a series of islands in the North Atlantic off North-west Europe that also includes Ireland. England is connected by land to Wales and Scotland, which lies to the north.

The Channel separates England from mainland Europe by a mere 20 miles of water, while the Irish Sea separates Wales and England from Ireland and the Atlantic separates us from the Americas. The North Sea separates England from Scandinavia and North-east Europe. England straddles the International Date Line at Greenwich, which gives us Greenwich Mean Time, and lies between 50 and 55 degrees north of the equator.

Getting to England and Wales is relatively easy. Honestly.

## By air

England and Wales are well served by dozens of airports, with Heathrow being a hub airport for world travel. There are lots of other regional airports, including major hubs at Manchester, Birmingham and Gatwick. Wales has a few very small airports, but they include Cardiff.

## By rail

The Channel Tunnel links Folkestone in Kent to Calais for road traffic on board the Eurotunnel Le Shuttle. It takes just about 35 minutes and there are four trains an hour. The train links up with the major French and English motorway networks.

www.eurotunnel.com

The Eurostar railway service uses the Channel Tunnel but is for foot passengers only, travelling from London to Paris, Brussels, the Alps or the South of France. There are connections in London for all English and Welsh railway stations, and the same is true for Paris and Brussels in Europe.

www.eurostar.com

## By sea

Ferries run to England from the following mainland Europe ports: Dunkirk, Calais, Dieppe, Cherbourg, Le Havre, St Malo and Roscoff to the south coast ports; Hook of Holland to Harwich; Zeebrugge and Rotterdam to Hull; and Amsterdam to Newcastle. Ferries from Ireland run to Holyhead, Fishguard and Pembroke Dock in West Wales as well as to Liverpool.

www.ferries.co.uk

## By road

As stated above, you can drive to England via the Channel Tunnel. If coming from Scotland, the major route is the M74, which links Glasgow and Edinburgh with Carlisle and the UK motorway network. Alternative routes exist on the A68 and the A1 via Berwick-upon-Tweed. There are other smaller roads, too.

# WHAT TO TAKE WITH YOU

**What are you going to take** with you on your epic trip around England and Wales? You're going to need a good night's sleep, some water to drink and some gas to cook on. Plus a load of other clobber. Got it all? Great.

## If you are renting a van

If you are renting a van or motorhome for your trip to England and Wales then you'll be limited by the amount you can carry in your luggage or cram into your car. However, do try and remember not to pack everything and the kitchen sink, especially when it comes to clothes. Space in camper vans can be limited, motorhomes less so, but even they aren't unlimited in cupboard space.

Some essentials will be provided by the rental company, so do check with them what they provide and what you'll need.

For a list of hire companies, see p346.

# Travelling with your own vehicle

Obviously you'll need some kit. No doubt you've got your own list of essentials, but in case you haven't, here's mine:

## Kit

**Hoses and universal adaptors** Water is essential, but it's not always easy to get it from the tap to the van. Carrying jerrycans is easy, but even so, a length of hose can get you out of all sorts of trouble. If you have a portable loo or on-board toilet a short length of hose can help you to clean it out. Keep it separately from the fresh-water hose. A set of Hozelock tap adaptors and a universal adaptor will make sure you can always fill up.

KIT LIST
- 10m (33ft) of flexible fresh-water fill-up hose
- Set of universal tap-to-hose adaptors
- 1m (3ft) length of hose for slopping out toilets

**Levelling chocks and spirit level** Some people can sleep on a slope, but I can't. So I *always* carry my levelling chocks. Recently I have acquired a mini two-plane spirit level that sits on the dashboard and tells me when I am getting close to level, but really a glass of water on a flat surface will do. And if you forget your chocks, a few copies of this book will do just as well.

KIT LIST
- 1 x set of Level Up levelling chocks
- 1 x spirit level

**Electric cables and extensions** If you have electric hook-up then you'll need a C Form or 16amp cable to go with it. A cable that is about 25m (80ft) is usually sufficient to reach any pitch. It may also be a good idea to carry a 13amp adaptor plug, as well as a 13amp socket if your campsite doesn't have a 16amp socket (though it should!).

**KIT LIST**
- 25m 16amp cable
- 13amp plug adaptor
- 13amp socket (to 16 amp)

**Wind-up torches and lamps** Wind-up torches are incredibly useful because they don't need any maintenance and don't create any waste. Some lanterns will charge up from the 12V socket in the van, so can always be kept topped up at no cost. Both are useful if you have to do a midnight loo stop.

**Spare gas canisters** Camping shops can be few and far between in some parts, so take a spare canister or two if you can. If you are running on LPG fill up *before* you head into the wild. Some stations do not supply it or may not have the right nozzle adaptor in the more remote corners of England or Wales.

**Solar panel** If you are going off-grid, a solar panel can trickle a charge into your leisure battery to stop it from running down, especially if you are running a lot of stuff off it. However, if you don't want to go to the hassle of fitting a larger one, consider running phones, lamps and gadgets off a portable solar charger.

**Maps maps maps** I always carry a map for route planning, as well as large-scale maps of the specific areas I am visiting so that I can get into the heart of the landscape.

OS 'Explorer' maps offer 1:25,000 scale and OS 'Landranger' maps offer 1:50,000 scale.

**Wet-weather gear** You never know in England and Wales. One minute it could be dry, the next it could be wetter than a wet weekend in Wembury. Be prepared with gear for any weather and hope you don't have to use it.

**Axe and firelighting equipment** You may not always get the chance to have a fire, but it's always worth carrying the kit for making it happen should the need arise. Just remember to avoid lighting fires in sensitive areas or on grass or where there is a danger of it spreading. If possible, take a fire pit too, then you can light up safely without damaging turf.

> **KIT LIST**
> - Axe
> - Firelighters/matches/fire steel
> - Firepit/wood/kindling

**Toilet kit** If you don't carry a portable loo then sooner or later you may have to indulge in a nature wee (or worse). Do not urinate within 30m (100ft) of any open waters, rivers or streams. If you do have to defecate, do it as far as possible from rivers, streams, buildings and animals. Dig a hole and bury it. Carry a trowel or folding spade.

> **KIT LIST**
> - Trowel
> - Cheap toilet paper (it tends to break down more easily)

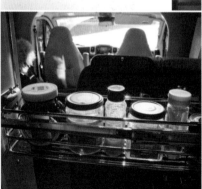

# EATING ON YOUR TRAVELS

I love my food. I really do. I like to try new food and I like to try local food. So every trip in the van has the potential to become a culinary adventure. You don't have to cook like a masterchef to enjoy the best of the ingredients on offer in England and Wales, nor do you have to have the deepest pockets to enjoy brilliant food prepared with love by the best chefs, although if you like posh restaurants it will help.

When you travel around the country you'll have the chance to try Welsh lamb, Anglesey sea salt, Dovedale cheese, Exmoor Jersey Blue cheese, Cornish clotted cream, Grimsby fish, Plymouth gin, Fenland celery and Lakeland Herdwick lamb precisely where they were raised, made or grown. That's really special, and I would implore anyone visiting our shores to try these regional products.

## Food that's protected locally

If you don't know where to start when it comes to buying local ingredients, it's worth checking the PDO (Protected Designation of Origin) status lists for foods that are made in the region you are visiting. These are lists of foods that have been given protected geographical status by the European Union. This means they cannot be made anywhere else. Like Champagne. Beyond the Champagne region of France, you cannot call sparkling wine Champagne. It's the same with the Cornish pasty (oh heavenly chow!), Arbroath smokies and Whitstable oysters.

21

## Local, fresh and seasonal

Buying local specialities will help the local economy (it's our way of giving back) as much as buying fresh local and seasonal foods from local shops (not supermarkets) will help to keep those growers and producers alive and kicking. The profit stays locally, and is worth a lot more than sending your pound straight to the pocket of some Surrey-based supermarket shareholder.

Local food is fresher, has travelled a shorter distance than a lot of food, often has less packaging (and less waste) and will almost always taste better.

## Eating out

Sometimes it can be tricky to know where to eat in England and Wales. Do you go for a restaurant or a pub?

Restaurants can be varied – especially in price – but you can't go wrong if you check out those Michelin stars (if your pocket can stand it) or Waitrose's *Good Food Guide* (www.thegoodfoodguide.co.uk). Sometimes you'll just have to go with your instinct. Does it look nice? Do you feel comfortable? Do you get a good welcome? Is it busy? (If it isn't, think twice!)

When it comes to pubs, it can be a lot more hit and miss, although of late things are changing. For many years the trend was towards a standard

set of pub grub dishes, with chips that were deep fried and would more or less sell themselves. Thankfully we've become a little more discerning over the years and now British food is enjoying a true, full-blown renaissance, with more chefs realising the value of local dishes cooked with love. The establishments have become known as 'gastropubs', which sounds great, although you might find your food served on something other than an actual plate, as many of them compete for the most imaginative presentation. If you don't believe me, check out wewantplates.com.

> **TIP**
> If in doubt, always have the local ham, egg and chips. It is so difficult to screw up this English favourite, although many have tried.

## Be generous if you can

There are motorhomers and camper-vanners who like to see how far their budget can stretch and who will happily brag about how little cash they have managed to spend on their travels. This is fine, but please remember that you contribute nothing to the local area if you camp wild, eat in with ingredients from the supermarket and don't buy anything when you are there. I assume you go there because you like it; therefore it seems to me that it makes sense to spend a bit of cash there to help it along after you've left.

# WHERE AND HOW TO STAY IN ENGLAND AND WALES

One of the best things about travelling in a motorhome or camper van is the ability to stop and have a sleep at the drop of your trousers. But finding somewhere safe, secure, pretty to look at and great to wake up in can sometimes be a challenge.

England and Wales have plenty of campsites, but you are not limited to them by any means. You can stay at Certificated Locations, on private land (with permission), in pub car parks, at motorhome overnight stops and even in some council car parks (bravo to those that allow it).

Before we get to the lowdown, remember this:

## Leave it nicer

Leave it nicer: it's your responsibility as a camper-van or motorhome owner. Wherever you lay your hat you have a duty to your fellow motorhome owners and to the world you inhabit. That is to keep

it tidy, to not make any mess and to be respectful. If you leave the place nicer than it was when you arrived you are making a positive contribution to that place – and you will be doing all other motorhomers and camper-vanners a favour at the same time. However, if you trash the place and leave a mess, you bugger it up for the rest of us.

- Tidy up your pitch when you arrive and before you leave
- Don't drop grey waste anywhere other than in designated places
- Use eco-friendly soaps, detergents and liquids
- Empty your chemical loo at designated points only
- Take your litter home
- Recycle as much as you can
- Buy and eat locally to contribute to the local economy
- Smile and be nice

25

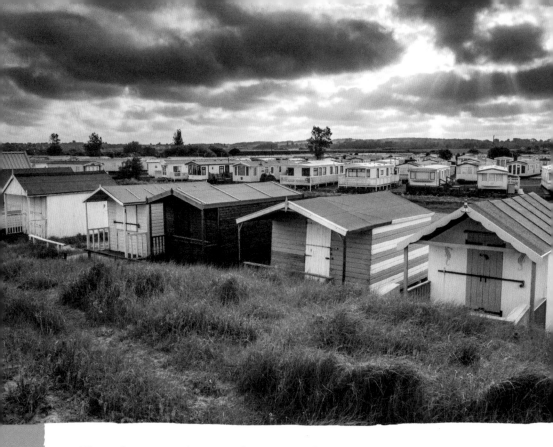

## Touring parks and campsites

England and Wales have a lot of campsites. From tiny sites to high-density touring parks and large, very well-organised Caravan and Motorhome Club or Camping and Caravanning Club sites, you have an awful lot of choice. Joining a club will get you a discounted rate at club sites, while a lot of the old-fashioned farmer's field sites may not have a website, never mind an online booking system. So you can play it any way you want to. My suggestion if you worry about finding a pitch but can't find something that's right for you before you get there would be to book the first couple of nights on a big site and then shop around when you get there.

There are lots of great online resources for finding sites too, such as Cool Camping and Campsited.

www.caravanclub.co.uk
www.campingandcaravanningclub.co.uk
www.pitchup.com
www.coolcamping.com
www.campsited.com

## Certificated Locations/Certificated Sites

These are small sites with a limited number of pitches. You can locate them with the handbook provided by either the Caravan and Motorhome Club or the Camping and Caravanning Club, or simply chance upon them as you drive. Either way, they offer the opportunity to camp in out-of-the-way sites, often in interesting locations. Often what they lack in terms of facilities (some may not even have loos or showers) they make up for in location.

www.caravanclub.co.uk
www.campingandcaravanningclub.co.uk

## Britstops

Based on the France Passion scheme, Britstops have been working hard to put growers, pub and restaurant owners, beauty spots, activity centres and farmers in touch with motorhomers by offering free overnight stops in exchange for nothing more than a smile and a wave and, hopefully, some business. There are hundreds of them all over England and Wales. I have to say that travelling in winter during the writing of this book was made easy by Britstops. When sites were closed we could always rely on a great pub with a warm fire to warm the cockles after a long day out in the snow. It's a great scheme and worthy of your money – you'll recoup the initial cost in no time.

The guidebook costs £27.50 and thereafter camping is free – just follow the code of conduct.

www.britstops.com

## 'Wild camping' spots

Wild camping is illegal in most of England and Wales. So that means you can't just turn up and expect a warm welcome. This is because most of the land is owned by someone, and to camp on it without permission is a civil offence. Even with the 'right to roam' and open access land in National Parks you do not have the right to park up where you please and camp overnight. On Dartmoor, where you can wild camp (in a tent), you cannot wild camp in a van or motorhome. The same applies in the Lake District, where lightweight camping above the treeline is OK. Your camper won't go up there.

But. And it is a big but. It is possible to wild camp (that is, park) in England and Wales if you know the right spot, are responsible and don't mind moving on if you have to. I have stayed overnight in my van in all kinds of places – lay-bys, motorway services, fields, lanes, beach car parks and remote parking areas – and never had any problem. But that doesn't mean it will be the same for you. I usually check with the landowner if I can find him or her, talk to people in the area about whether it's OK and generally try to tidy up when I arrive and before I leave. This is one way of answering the critics before they get started. People are afraid you'll stay for ages and will leave a mess. And everyone who does that ruins it for the rest of us.

So, to mitigate, we try to change hearts and minds by being nice, sensible, good-hearted campers.

Don't ignore 'no overnight parking' signs.
Be respectful.

## Motorhome stopovers

Some councils and private individuals have got the wherewithal to realise that motorhomers can be good for business and that to welcome them is to welcome a potential new revenue stream. UK Motorhomes lists places where motorhomes can park up overnight in car parks, pubs and public spaces. See their list at:

www.ukmotorhomes.net/uk-stopovers

Motorhome stopover, not dissimilar to Britstops, is a scheme that puts motorhomers together with pub and car park owners.

www.motorhomestopover.co.uk

## Why some councils could be missing a trick

How many beach car parks sit empty overnight? A lot. But we're not allowed to stay on them. Why? Because local residents don't like it and councils don't want the hassle, mess or disturbance. Fair enough. Some motorhomers have been guilty of causing all of these. But what if we paid – a tenner, say – to stay overnight, made sure the place was tidy and contributed to keeping the toilets open and clean? What if we showed the world that we are decent, law-abiding people who just want to enjoy the view and don't mind paying for the privilege? Would councils see it differently then? I am sure they would. Especially when you consider that most motorhomers will also contribute to the local economy by buying fuel, food and drinks whenever they stay anywhere.

Councils have the power to grant overnight licences for their car parks. They could be enjoying a new revenue stream in tough times. But no, many of them fear the loss of business that this would cause to local campsites and guest houses, which is a misguided fear, simply because most motorhomers don't want to stay on a campsite *every* night. So they up sticks and go elsewhere, taking their business away from the area. If, however, they were allowed to stay a couple of nights in the car park by the beach, they might then stay on a local campsite for a night to refresh themselves and charge the tanks, so bringing *more* business instead of less to the local area.

Councillors, think about it. And well done to Torridge in North Devon, which already does this.

# THE SOUTH WEST

England's South West, which
includes Bristol, Somerset, Dorset, Devon and
Cornwall, is just about perfect for a slow road adventure.
It has open country, open beaches and open skies that will take
your breath away. From Glastonbury Tor to the wooded combes
of North Devon it has a host of marvels: waterfalls, rocky valleys,
cathedrals, granite tors and magnificent lighthouses. Both coasts offer
long-distance driving routes: the A39 from Minehead in Somerset
to Padstow in Cornwall can be driven in one long, gorgeous
trundle, while Exeter is the starting point for a merry
pootle to Portland Bill. All you have to do is drive.

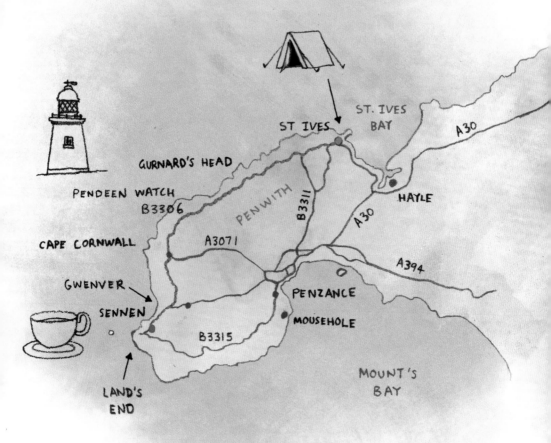

ST. IVES BAY

A30

ST IVES

GURNARD'S HEAD

PENDEEN WATCH
B3306

PENWITH

B3311

HAYLE

A30

CAPE CORNWALL

A3071

A394

GWENVER

SENNEN

PENZANCE

MOUSEHOLE

B3315

LAND'S
END

MOUNT'S
BAY

# ROUTE 01

# ST IVES TO SENNEN

## A SLOW ROAD IN THE LAND OF SAINTS

A coastal route that takes in one of Cornwall's best-loved towns, some top-notch art establishments, a lot of very beautiful coastline, ancient sites and a few hidden, and very pretty, beaches. The route also passes through the Cornish Mining World Heritage Site, a unique post-industrial landscape perched high on a clifftop.

BEST FOR:
**Beaches, surf, art and culture**

START: **St Ives**

END: **Sennen**

MILEAGE: **18 miles (29 kilometres)**

DAYS TO EXPLORE: **1**

OS LANDRANGER MAP: **203**

THE SOUTH WEST

33

It's January, but from the view from inside the van, as I wipe the condensation from the side window, it could be high summer, despite a few fast-moving clouds above. The sun is shining on St Ives below us and the sea is blue, except for a few patches that are darkened by cloud-shaped shadows. The light, as it is so often here in this part of Cornwall, is piercing, illuminating sand and sea and the cottages, sail lofts and bungalows that make up the town with a bright and sharp glow.

We see the Tate Gallery on Porthmeor Beach, home to the work of local artists brought here in droves by that penetrating brightness. They came for the life and light, and from our pitch at Ayr Holiday Park we can see why. The views of the town are unfettered by buildings or trees or even other campers. We've been kept warm overnight by a fan heater and were kept entertained last evening by a swim in the pool, a sauna and a few too many minutes in the steam room. But that's camping in January, I suppose. You take the heat wherever you can get it.

The surf looks small but clean, and very definitely surfable, so we breakfast quickly and then pack up the van and head down the hill to the beach. Despite the time of year the sea actually looks inviting, so we rush in, immersing ourselves in the cold, clear water. Surfing at this time of the year is always invigorating, exciting, life affirming, especially in bright sunshine. We might be covered from head to toe in neoprene and hence warm, but the cold spray on our faces reminds us of the time of the year. At times it stings a little. Surfing in winter can be harsh, but so liberating.

We surf – and laugh – for an hour or so, then prepare to head south towards Sennen Cove. But before we can get out of our wetsuits a dark cloud, with accompanying breeze, whips up the surf and brings a sudden downpour of rain that's as sharp as the light. Our skin breaks into goose bumps as we remove our wetsuits, standing in puddles, somehow staying

dry enough to pull on our clothes. We shelter under the tailgate, waiting for the clouds to pass before running around the van clearing up wetsuit boots and accessories, and stuffing boards into board bags as quickly as we can.

We're steamed up by the time we drive up and out of town on the B3306 so we turn up the fan heater to full blast. I am very glad to be in a T5 rather than in my old T2. Winter camping is always tricky, but in the T2 it was particularly tough.

The road is clear, with the exception of a few farm vehicles and the odd motorhome, and so the driving is good. We take our time, enjoying the twists and turns and stopping to look at views and take notes and photographs. At Pendeen we watch the choughs below us tumble and whirl on the wind as the spray drifts up the cliffs like smoke. We hike down to Portheras Cove for our picnic lunch. The water colour belies the season and we consider a dip, but no, not today. Not in our smalls. At Cape Cornwall we trail our fingers in the tidal pool, wondering again if we dare strip and dip, like we normally would, taking shrieking leaps into the wind-rippled water. But, unlike at Portheras, it actually looks cold, so we back away and tramp back up the hill to the van. We stand at the top of the steep sandy cliff at Gwenver Beach and I tell Liz about the first time I came here: how friends and I discovered it on a surf trip in the 1990s and thought we'd found heaven, or at least a place as close to California as we could imagine. That would have been heaven enough. At Sennen we scoff cake and coffee with a view of the beach in front of us and a wood burner to warm our hands. It's perfect, a best-day-ever kind of day, on one of Britain's best driving routes. We head back to St Ives.

At Carn Galver we stop to look at the ruins of the engine house. It's 3 p.m. and the light is changing fast, growing more amber by the minute. The wind is colder too, the temperature dropping fast. Even so, I manage to badger Liz into climbing Carn Galver itself, the rocky hill behind the engine house. At just 229m (751ft) above sea level it's an easy hike across spongy peat and heather, although we have to clamber a little over the piles of lichen-covered granite at the top. When we turn to savour the view it's breathtaking, in more ways than one. The wind is stronger and colder up here and the views towards Land's End are lovely. The winter colours are stunning, ranging from deep green grass to the grey greens and silvers of the granite, contrasting with the sparkling battleship grey of the sea and the oranges and purples of the died-back bracken and heather. We see the

field systems, the way the coastal strip has been cultivated over time, the way the cliffs drop steeply into the sea and the way the road snakes its way between hamlets. On the east side of the road the landscape is in its natural form – wild, rough and tough – while on the west side it's been shaped by man, the engine house a monument to past endeavours. We smell peat and salt and spray and feel the wind's cool prickles on our faces as the sun drops below the clouds. Liz gets up from her perch on the tor and runs back down the hill, to the warmth of the van and the comfort of our home on wheels. I snap a last shot and follow her back down to the van, then it's back to the B3306, at the end of the weekend, and the end of another amazing slow road adventure.

# THE DRIVING

The B3306 is one of Britain's most beautiful driving roads. From a first glance of the map you might wonder why it should be given such an accolade. It doesn't have dizzying drops, steep ascents, wheel-spinning hairpins, high passes or challenging corners. It isn't even that long. In fact, it's one of the shortest routes in this book. At just over 16 miles from its artsy start in St Ives to its final coffee-and-cake-fuelled conclusion at the beach in Sennen, it's nothing more than a wee pootle, but what it lacks in length it makes up for in wallop.

You might meet all kinds of other road users on this stretch during the busy season, but don't be afraid to dawdle, even if you spy the tailback building up in your rear-view mirror. Not only will your lack of speed annoy the hell out of the middle-aged boy racers in their Audi TTs who come here to 'challenge themselves', but it may also cause mild annoyance to the bikers who white line it here. Cyclists, of course, will love your careful attention to their lives because you'll be the one type of road user who isn't out to kill them.

The point of driving a road like the B3306 is not to hare along it at a hundred miles an hour, although many try. The point is to savour the views, stop and take note of history, find hidden coves and beaches of paradise, seek out the choughs flapping madly in the breeze and enjoy the wilder side

of Cornwall, because it doesn't get much more wild than this.

From St Ives, the B3306 heads west, past the Leach Pottery and out of the town. Almost immediately you hit rural West Penwith, a land of ancients, where a sea of fern and granite, ordered only by crumbling walls or the timeworn grooves of medieval tilling, drops down into a churning blue sea. Steaming swells hit tough, stoic cliffs, while above, carns rise gently above the fields beyond the narrow strip of agriculture.

This area of Cornwall has more ancient monuments and sites than any other place in Britain. This is truly the land of saints and mysteries. There are quoits and standing stones, circles and Iron Age villages. Once you are up high, enjoying the view from the top of a rock and peat carn, you can see the scars of ancient field systems on the clifftops.

Leaving St Ives, the road meanders into this ancient countryside, following the contours of the land below the hills and above the fields, dodging between granite farm buildings in sharp turns. Between the grass-topped Cornish hedges, the cottages appear to grow from the earth itself, made as they are from the rocks in the fields, their low stone lintels and peeling paint inviting those who pass by to look, or at least to indulge in a fleeting fantasy of a life of escape from the maddening world.

Most notable among the buildings on this stretch of road are ruined tin and copper mine workings from the 19th century. At one time two thirds of the world's copper was exported from West Penwith. Today the engine houses lie in partial ruins, with the exception of the Levant beam engine house, which has been restored and remains working, under steam, of course. Along the cliffs, particularly at St Just, Botallack and Pendeen, you can see these engine houses perched on the edges of the cliffs. Their shafts, now grated to save the foolhardy from falling, plunge down as deep as 600m (1,968ft) and spread out under the sea for over one kilometre (3,280ft).

I have loved driving the B3306 for over 30 years. I used to be frustrated with its curves and contours in the days when I'd be looking to make the most of a narrow window of opportunity with a surf at Sennen Cove after a day of working in the surf shop at St Ives. I'd grow weary of the tootling tourists as I missed out on the tiny coves, hared past the villages and ignored the side roads to tiny hamlets and the walks up to the views above the road. Don't be me when you come here. Take your time. Stop along the way as you pass through Zennor, Pendeen, Botallack and St Just. Make time to drive down to Cape Cornwall, once thought to be the most westerly point in England. There's a small tidal pool at the wrongly named Priest's Cove just below the cape that's just begging for you to dive in. You can walk along the coast path to explore the ruins or stop to admire the swells slamming into the cliffs below. Catching sight of the Cornish chough flapping wildly against the wind is a thrill, even if you're not an ornithologist. They are rare companions on these lively, lonely cliffs.

St Just is the only other significant town on the B3306 besides St Ives. It was once the centre of the Cornish mining industry, and its granite cottages retain an end-of-the-world vigour. If you were ever to move here, you couldn't budge it if you tried, you could only adapt, and that's why it's so lovely.

From St Just, the B3306 takes a few final twists and turns before rising up to the flat plains of Land's End. A long straight will take you past Land's End Airport, the departure point for the Scillies, if you wanted to push further into the Atlantic. Past the airfield, the B3306 joins up with the A30 for the last

couple of miles before Land's End. Don't give up just yet, though. A turn off to the right will take you to the unimaginably beautiful Gwenver Beach, a stretch of silver sand and a deep blue sea. It's one of those places that will move you, I promise. I can still remember the first time I found it, way back in 1986. You won't forget it either.

Once on the A30 you can either potter on towards Land's End or drop down the hill to Sennen. I'd go for the hillier option and take in the sea air at this other lovely beach. Park above the beach and take tea and cake at the Ben Tunnicliffe restaurant.

Then go and dip your toes.

## PLACES TO STAY

**Ayr Holiday Park**
Alexandra Road, St Ives, Cornwall, TR26 1EJ
**web:** www.ayrholidaypark.co.uk
**tel:** 01736 795855

**info:** *Few campsites have locations like this, overlooking St Ives and Porthmeor Beach. Book early!*

**Secret Garden Caravan & Camping Park**
Bosavern House, St Just, Penzance, Cornwall, TR19 7RD
**web:** www.secretbosavern.com
**email:** mail@bosavern.com
**tel:** 01736 788301

**info:** *A small, friendly site within a walled garden near St Just. Book early to get one of just 12 pitches.*

# IN THE AREA

**Tate St Ives** One of the Tate Gallery family, with permanent exhibitions of St Ives School painters, plus travelling exhibitions. Fantastic position overlooking Porthmeor Beach.
• www.tate.org.uk/visit/tate-st-ives

**Barbara Hepworth Museum and Sculpture Garden** Barbara Hepworth was one of the UK's best-known sculptors. She moved to St Ives in 1949 and set up a home and studio at Trewyn Studio. She worked there until her death in 1975. Today the studio and garden are open to the public, with a permanent collection of her work on display. • www.barbarahepworth.org.uk/st-ives

**Levant Mine and Beam Engine** A working beam engine, plus mine workings at one of West Penwith's greatest mine operations, at the heart of Cornwall's Cornish Mining World Heritage Site. • www.nationaltrust.org.uk/levant-mine-and-beam-engine

**Geevor Tin Mine** The largest preserved mine site in the country, and an opportunity to go underground into an 18th-century tin mine. • www.geevor.com

## Nearest van hire

**Kernow Kampers**
• www.kernow-campers.com

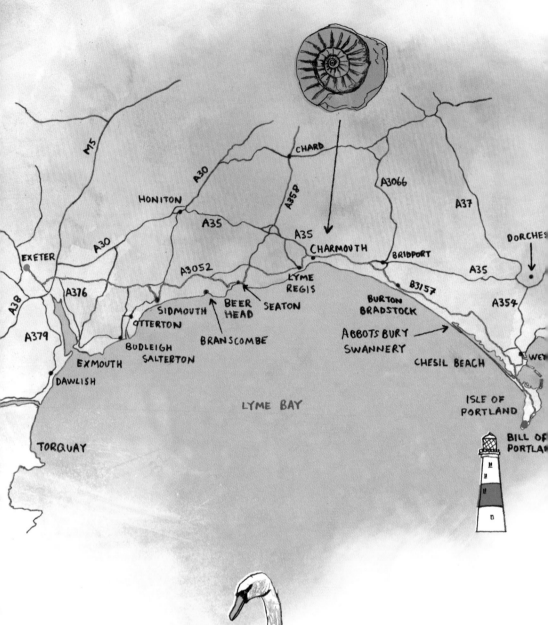

M5

A30

HONITON

A35

A358

CHARD

A3066

A37

A30

EXETER

A376

A38

A379

A3052

SIDMOUTH

OTTERTON

BUDLEIGH
SALTERTON

EXMOUTH

DAWLISH

TORQUAY

BEER
HEAD

BRANSCOMBE

SEATON

LYME
REGIS

A35

CHARMOUTH

BRIDPORT

B3157

BURTON
BRADSTOCK

ABBOTSBURY
SWANNERY

CHESIL BEACH

A35

A354

DORCHES

WE

LYME BAY

ISLE OF
PORTLAND

BILL OF
PORTLA

# ROUTE 02

# EXETER TO PORTLAND BILL

## BEACH HUT BILL

Crossing the 'border' from Devon to Dorset along the coast is a fabulous coastal jaunt that takes in tiny villages, big beaches, tall cliffs and even the odd film location. The contrast, between the tidy, cosy seaside towns of Devon and the desolate, end-of-the-world feel that a windy day on Portland can give you, couldn't be greater.

BEST FOR:
**Wild and windy walks on Portland Bill**

START: **Exeter**

END: **Portland Bill**

MILEAGE: **65 miles (105 kilometres)**

DAYS TO EXPLORE: **2**

OS LANDRANGER MAP: **192, 193, 194**

THE SOUTH WEST

45

I park by the lighthouse at Portland Bill. It's one of those red-and-white-striped affairs, a classic design that stands 41m (134ft) tall. If I was a kid again – trust me, I try constantly – this is the way I'd draw a lighthouse. It stands on the promontory overlooking the English Channel, supervising ships as they navigate the Shambles sandbank and the Portland tidal race, which we can see offshore in the bright blue water, churning up the surface into whitecaps.

The Portland stone on which the lighthouse is built has a beautiful light grey and creamy hue, which is what makes it famous the world over and which is also why it was chosen by architects for lots of famous landmarks, including St Paul's Cathedral.

We walk to the east of the lighthouse to see some of the old quarrying works and take a look at Red Crane, the steel crane that was once used to lower stone into boats and that is now used to lower boats. We walk along the edge of the cliff, looking down at the slabs of rock below us. They lie

flat, with a series of drop-offs leading to the sea. There are occasional patches of sand between the boulders at the base of the cliffs. It's creamy and light, just like the stone. We guess that the heavy weight of this type of stone is the reason the water is so clear: softer rocks usually mean silty seas and no visibility. That must also be one of the reasons that diving in the waters off Portland – and Dorset in general – is some of the best in the UK.

We continue to walk eastwards, away from the lighthouse and towards a block of ramshackle huts on the cliff edge. They are arranged in half a dozen rough 'squares' in the scrub grassland close to the cliff edge. It's a cool day so they are all locked up, put away until later in the year, like thrift planted on top of low stone walls, hidden away until it's time to bloom. The place feels forgotten, like everyone just packed up and left, a *Dr Who* location abandoned after filming.

The huts are in various states. Some are brightly painted, some that typical dour dark shade of garden shed brown. Some have jolly names evoking warm places far away or sunny states of mind, while others have little annexes or solar panels. I focus on a dark green hut with a peeling felt roof and a bright red door. The paint flakes off – some might call this weathered look a patina – as the wind blows and the heads of the coastal grasses bob with the gusts. It has a solar panel on the roof that, we fear, wouldn't be enough to boil a kettle on a day like this. I take a picture. I love to come to places like this when it's out of season because it's a bit ... well ...

moody. The wind blows mournfully through the roofing felt, and I'll bet it's colder inside than out.

I read later that a couple who lease one of the huts will lose their bricks-and-mortar home after a row with the landlords who own the land the huts are on left them with a legal bill of £100K and saw them evicted from their precious weekend retreat. With planning permission already granted to the owner – and former mayor – for new huts, which may sell for up to £35,000, on the sites of the old ones, it looks as if Portland is heading for gentrification. I for one will be a little sad when the money moves in, if it does. Portland is a wild little corner, and its ramshackle heart is in the flaking wooden doors and one-pot solar panels. It's England: tatty and a bit tired, braving the weather, putting a brew on, sitting out the storm on the edge of Europe, bragging about the old days and having a whinge about the landlord.

Shall we make England great again? Nah. Let's put the kettle on and patch up this leaky old ceiling.

# THE DRIVING

Portland is the final stop on a brilliant drive along the south coast from Exeter, along the A3052 and then the A35 and B3157 and, finally, the A354. Starting out from Exeter, the journey takes a little time to wind up to its full value, but it's an easy run into Sidmouth as your first detour. The B3176 will take you into this beautiful Regency town to enjoy its short prom jammed in between tall red cliffs. Then it's up and out again on the A375 for the short hop to Beer, another tiny Devon village that's worth a brief stop for fudge or ice cream. Seaton is next, then you're on the way to Lyme Regis and its famous Cobb sea wall. It's a squeeze to park, but a walk down the hill will do you good anyway, if you have the patience. Charmouth is the next stop for eagle-eyed dinosaur hunters, who will love it all the more after a storm as that's when the best stuff gets washed out from the muddy cliffs. It's a great place to stop.

The A35 will whisk you elegantly over more Dorset hills, eventually becoming the Bridport bypass, where you'll have to make a quick right turn on the B3157 towards West Bay (if you want to see the place where they filmed *Broadchurch*) and Burton Bradstock for a ride across beautiful rolling countryside and up to the top of Abbotsbury Hill. This is one of the high points of the journey, when you get to see Chesil Beach stretch off into the distance, with Portland at the end.

The B3157 continues on down the hill, through the tiny (narrow) village at Abbotsbury, on to Portesham and then into Weymouth, which can get a bit convoluted, but if you follow the B3156 to the A354 you'll find yourself crossing the narrow isthmus that makes up the west side of Portland Harbour.

Once you're on Portland, it's hard to get lost. Follow signs in Fortuneswell up the hill to Weston and then on to Portland Bill, where you'll find the lighthouse and the beach huts.

## PLACES TO STAY

**Wood Farm Camping and Caravanning**
Charmouth, Dorset, DT6 6BT
**web:** www.woodfarm.co.uk
**email:** reception@woodfarm.co.uk
**tel:** 01297 560697

**info:** *A big site in the rolling hills behind Charmouth Beach. Luckily it's terraced, with good pitches and a pool. Yes, a pool! Very handy for fossil hunting on Charmouth Beach.*

**East Fleet Farm Touring Park**
Chickerell, Weymouth, Dorset, DT3 4DW
**web:** www.eastfleet.co.uk
**email:** enquiries@eastfleet.co.uk
**tel:** 01305 785768

**info:** *A Caravan and Motorhome Club Site on the shores of the Fleet Lagoon, just west of Portland. Standard-issue quality, of course, in a touring park.*

**Sea Barn Farm**
Fleet, Weymouth, Dorset, DT3 4ED
**web:** www.seabarnfarm.co.uk
**email:** enquire@seabarnfarm.co.uk
**tel:** 01305 782218

**info:** *With great views of Portland and the coast, there's another sunset to savour at this well-organised camping park.*

# IN THE AREA

**Abbotsbury Swannery**  If you like swans but don't like cages, then Abbotsbury could be the perfect day out for you! This swan sanctuary has been going since the 10th century, although these days the birds aren't fattened up for eating. One of Dorset's best days out.
• **www.abbotsbury-tourism.co.uk/swannery**

**Charmouth Heritage Coast Centre**  Dinosaurs are the name of the game at Charmouth, the centre of the Jurassic Coast experience. Go for a dinosaur-hunting tour, borrow a hammer or look at the miracles that have been taken out of the cliffs at the museum. Well worth a peek, especially after storms.  • **www.charmouth.org/chcc**

**The Weymouth and Portland National Sailing Academy**  Built for the 2012 Olympics and now housing lots of schools and training providers, this could be the best place to learn how to sail, windsurf or stand-up paddleboarding in Britain.  • **www.wpnsa.org.uk**

**The Jurassic Skyline**  For a bird's eye view of the coast, Weymouth's Jurassic Skyline will take you up 174 feet (53m) into the air above Weymouth Harbour in a revolving gondola. A bit like the good old days of the Post Office Tower but not.
• **www.jurassicskyline.com**

Nearest van hire

**South West Camper Hire Ltd**
• www.swcamperhire.com

BRISTOL CHANNEL

VALLEY OF THE ROCKS

LYNMOUTH

LYNTON

ILFRACOMBE    LEE ABBEY    FORELAND POINT

WOOLACOMBE

MORTE
POINT

BAGGY
POINT

SAUNTON

BRAUNTON

A399

A3123

WATERSMEET

PORLOCK    MINEHEAD

BRIDGWATER
BAY

BURNHAM
ON-SEA

WATCHET

WHEDDON
CROSS

A39

QUANTOCK
HILLS

BRIDGWATER

EXMOOR

NATIONAL

PARK

SOMERSET

BARNSTAPLE

BRAYFORD

A361

A39

BIDEFORD

SOUTH
MOLTON

BAMPTON

TAUNTON

A377

A361

B3231

DEVON

M5

# ROUTE 03

# THE EXMOOR COAST

## ON THE EDGE

The Exmoor Coast is simply stunning. From pretty Minehead to Barnstaple, it's a roller coaster of a ride with deep valleys, steep drops, lovely beaches and some absolutely cracking driving. Go any time of the year for drama, in the summer for beaches and in the winter for bleakness. A coast for all seasons.

BEST FOR:
**Stunning coastal views**

START: M5 Junction 23 Bridgwater

END: Barnstaple

MILEAGE: 85 miles (136 kilometres)

DAYS TO EXPLORE: 4

OS LANDRANGER MAP: 180, 181, 182

THE SOUTH WEST

We are heading home to Bude, taking a detour along the north coast. The usual way to get home is to blatt along the A361 to Barnstaple or take the M5 as far as Exeter, then the A30. But that's just soulless and not much fun at all. It's perfunctory, like eating for fuel, not pleasure.

It's a joy to be on the road today because it's our first outing since the winter and the leaves have just come out on the trees. Blackthorn blossom is in the hedgerows and there are bright green leaves on the trees as we cruise into Porlock. It's late afternoon and the sun is cooling off. Porlock Weir is beautiful but in shadow by the time we pull up at the car park to take pictures.

Leaving the tiny collection of houses at the weir we have two choices: we can go up Porlock Hill or we can take the toll road through the private estate. Porlock Hill is notoriously steep and will get us up on to the top of Exmoor a lot more quickly, while the toll road will cost us a few quid and take longer. I think of my grandfather, who used to drive this road with his brother in the 1920s before the A30 or A361 were built. They came down to Devon from Totteridge in London, to paint and draw, but also to tackle Porlock Hill. In the early days of motoring, Porlock was the prize they all wanted. My grandfather used to tell me how they took it on in reverse sometimes as that was the only way they'd get their old Standard 10 up there. At 1 in 4 in places, it's the steepest A road in Britain, but not the most interesting. So while he might turn in his grave at the thought of me taking the easy way out, I turn right before the hairpin and take the toll road.

I am glad I did. As the road rises out of the village the views are incredible looking back at Somerset, Porlock and the flat country we've just pootled through. We pass through dense forest of hornbeam, pine and oak, snaking around tight turns, following the contours of the hillside. Occasionally a clearing shows us another view and we stop to look. This is just fabulous, and while I have driven this route many times, I see it now as a delight rather than a slow inconvenience that gets in the way of a holiday. It's a joy to drive such a twisted long way around, even though it costs us £3 for the privilege.

At the top we emerge from the shadows to be greeted by a sunny Exmoor, and are stopped by a group of shaggy, tough-looking Exmoor ponies. They saunter across the road as if they owned the place, which they probably do.

We make our way across the moor in the late-afternoon sun and stop at the top of Countisbury Hill, the sharp drop into Lynmouth. I get out of the van and peer over the edge. It's incredibly steep and the sea is a few hundred feet below us. I tell Lizzy about one of the times I drove this route, on the way home from a surf trip in the late eighties. I had been surfing

at Putsborough and wanted to get in the sea before it got too dark. It was January. I jumped in the sea at Lynmouth and paddled out to the waves, which break there over a rocky river mouth. Despite paddling hard, I was swept away to the east in the current and found myself below a huge cliff, sitting on my board, in the water. I couldn't paddle back to the beach, so I managed to beach myself on a narrow strip of sand beneath the cliff. I climbed the cliff and sat on a rock, with my board across my knees, watching the sea below me, unable to go up or down. The cliff was too steep to climb. I couldn't see anything of the beach, just the sea, with the lights of South Wales twinkling opposite me. As the light faded I realised I had to do something or I'd have to sit there until the tide went out again.

I climbed down to the sandy strip, timing my final leap to coincide with the drawing back of the waves. When the next wave came in, I climbed the cliff again to avoid being dashed on the rocks. I did this a few times until I could see the last corner of the beach before me, then one last dash between waves and I was home and dry. My friends, who were waiting on the beach, were about to call the coastguard. I got a telling off.

We leave Lynmouth and head up to the Valley of the Rocks, an extraordinary valley with sheer cliffs on one side and tor-like formations of rock balancing on the precipice. Then we follow the road to Lee Abbey and the toll road to Woody Bay and on to the A39. It's another unmissable ride, even narrower than before, but stunning, with great views over the rocky coves below. It's slow going, but who cares?

# THE DRIVING

The north section of the A39, between the M5 at Junction 23 and Barnstaple, is one hell of a road. It's not the best way to get into North Devon, but it is by far the prettiest. The further you go the better it gets, offering fabulous slow-road offshoots and follies, and a couple of teeny-weeny toll roads that are definitely worth checking out.

Come off the M5 at Junction 23 and head south into Bridgwater, following signs for the A39, Watchet and Minehead. The first part of the journey, east of Bridgwater, you're still on the levels of Somerset so the driving isn't so exciting, but don't despair: it will soon get better as you begin to rise into the Quantock Hills, when the road begins to twist and turn. Dropping down from the Quantocks towards Exmoor there are some very fine views to the west. Dunster is the next stop, and the castle can easily be seen from the road. It's worth a stop by the meadows to get a good view. Despite having a reputation as a Butlins resort, Minehead is a lovely little town, with an interesting – and long – past. It also marks the start of the South West Coast Path. From Minehead the A39 rises to Porlock and then drops again to bring you to the foot of Porlock Hill. Before you decide whether to take the steep 1 in 4 ascent or the winding toll road, nip down to the weir for a pint and a wander. It's really lovely down there and there is plenty of parking.

If you go for the toll road, you'll find your way up to the top of Exmoor via a series of sharp bends that give tantalising glimpses of the sea and Porlock between the trees. It's an exciting road, narrow in places, but at least not as steep at the main road. At the top you'll pay the toll, then meet up with the main road, the A39. Then it's on towards Lynmouth via Countisbury. This is a truly spectacular part, so do take the time to stop and admire the views, ponies and the steep wooded combes below you. A walk will take you to Foreland Point and the lighthouse, which feels very isolated. Countisbury Hill, which slides very quickly into Lynmouth, is another steep drop, but it's worth it as the views are incredible. Once in Lynmouth, take the road for Lynmouth and the Valley of the Rocks. This wonderful valley is a natural wonder, a clifftop valley with steep rocky towers and drops. Stop here if you're in a small van and admire the views, then head back to the A39 at Barbrook. If you are in a little van, continue on through the valley to Lee Abbey and the toll road to Woody Bay. It's narrow and steep in places, with dizzying drops to the sea, so it's not suitable for bigger vans and motorhomes (NO, IT ISN'T). Join the A39 again at Woody Bay station. Carry on along the A39 until you get to Blackmoor Gate, then take a right on the A399 towards Combe Martin. This is the village with the longest high street in England and the highest sea cliff. They do good strawberries too – and supplied some of the gold in the crown jewels!

After that you're off to Ilfracombe via Watermouth Castle and the lovely Watermouth Bay. Then it's the much maligned but seriously beautiful town of Ilfracombe with its celebration of womanhood by Damien Hirst standing tall on the quayside. A diversion will take you to Lee Bay and Mortehoe on little roads, but you can whizz on straight to Woolacombe on the A39 and then on the B3343. Woolacombe is a fabulous little beach town with a clean beach, great surf and a lovely laid-back vibe. You can head back up the hill and then carry on to

Braunton or you can see the best of North Devon by heading up the steep hill out of Woolacombe towards Georgeham and Croyde. This will bring you into picturesque and popular Croyde village, then round Downend Point towards Saunton Beach, into Saunton on the B3231 and on to Braunton.

The views along the B3231 are astounding and there is a handy lay-by. Braunton is the place to stop and shop for surf gear and cake before heading towards Barnstaple, the final stop.

## PLACES TO STAY

### North Morte Farm Caravan & Camping Park
Mortehoe, Woolacombe, Devon, EX34 7EG
**web:** www.northmortefarm.co.uk
**email:** info@northmortefarm.co.uk
**tel:** 01271 870381

**info:** *A fabulous family-run site on a clifftop with direct beach access in the cutesy village of Mortehoe.*

### Ocean Pitch Campsite
Moor Lane, Croyde, Devon, EX33 1NZ
**web:** www.oceanpitch.co.uk
**email:** oceanpitchcroyde@gmail.com
**tel:** 07581024348

**info:** *A beach side campsite in Croyde with amazing views of one of the UK's nicest beaches.*

### Putsborough Sands Caravan Park
Putsborough, Braunton, Devon, EX33 1LB
**web:** www.putsborough.com
**email:** rob@putsborough.com
**tel:** 01271 890231/07774 887952

**info:** *Camper vans and motorhomes only at the beach at Putsborough. Great surf and a great beach with 3 miles of sand to play on.*

### Sunny Lyn Holiday Park
Lynbridge, Lynton, Devon, EX35 6NS
**web:** www.sunnylyn.co.uk
**email:** info@sunnylyn.co.uk
**tel:** 01598 753384

**info:** *A really well situated site on the river just inland from Lynmouth. Great for walking.*

# IN THE AREA

**The Lynton and Lynmouth Cliff Railway**  This fabulously quirky attraction put the fun back into funicular. A water-powered cliff railway that's a shortcut between Lynton and Lynmouth.  • **www.cliffrailwaylynton.co.uk**

**Watermouth Castle**  It's a castle and a theme park with a bonkers water-powered organ thingy that makes fountains to music. Plus lots of other rides and oddities.  • **www.watermouthcastle.com**

**Museum of British Surfing**  A tiny museum in Braunton that's packed with great stuff telling the story of surfing in Britain.  • **www.museumofbritishsurfing.org.uk**

**Watersmeet Lynmouth**  A really beautifully situated former fishing lodge and National Trust property at the place where the East and West Lyn rivers meet.  • **www.nationaltrust.org.uk/watersmeet**

**The South West Coast Path**  It begins at Minehead and covers 630 miles to Studland in Dorset. Great, challenging, inspiring walking. England's highest sea cliff is on this section at Combe Martin.  • **www.southwestcoastpath.org.uk**

### Nearest van hire

**coast2coast Camper Hire**
 • www.coast2coastcamperhire.co.uk

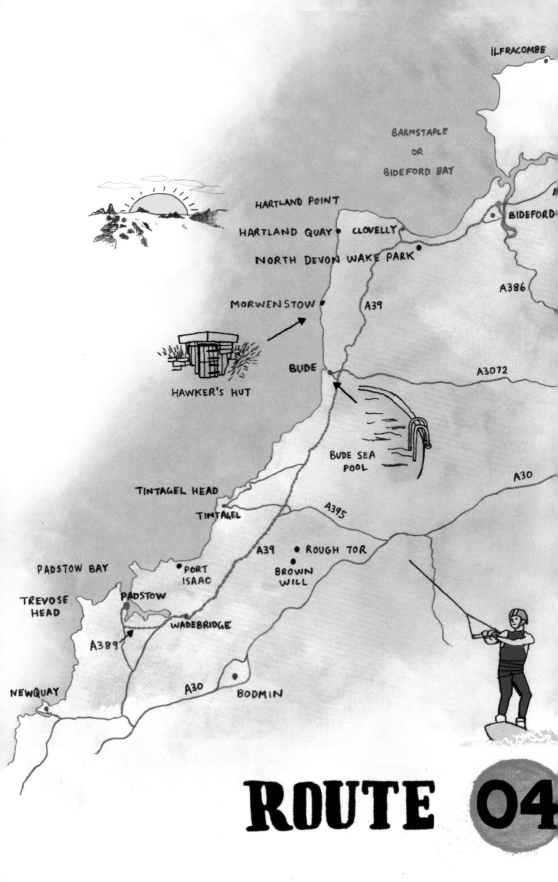

ILFRACOMBE

BARNSTAPLE
OR
BIDEFORD BAY

HARTLAND POINT

HARTLAND QUAY • CLOVELLY

NORTH DEVON WAKE PARK

BIDEFORD

A386

MORWENSTOW

A39

HAWKER'S HUT

BUDE

A3072

BUDE SEA
POOL

A30

TINTAGEL HEAD

TINTAGEL

A395

A39 • ROUGH TOR

PADSTOW BAY

PORT
ISAAC

BROWN
WILL

TREVOSE
HEAD

PADSTOW

WADEBRIDGE

A389

NEWQUAY

A30

BODMIN

# ROUTE 04

ROUTE 04

# THE ATLANTIC HIGHWAY

## LIFE IN THE COMBES

The Atlantic Highway is North Devon and Cornwall's answer to America's Pacific Coast Highway. And while it might be easy to joke that it's not quite up to the same standard because it doesn't run along the shoreline at all, it's still a brilliant road, with lovely views and opportunities for getting off the beaten track all along its glorious 60 miles between Bideford and Padstow.

BEST FOR:
**Exploring tiny coves and hidden beaches**

START: **Bideford**

END: **Padstow**

MILEAGE: **60 miles (97 kilometres) if direct**

DAYS TO EXPLORE: **3**

OS LANDRANGER MAP: **180, 190, 200**

THE SOUTH WEST

65

It's hot and sunny, with barely a whisper of wind. We're off exploring, map on the dash, surfboards on the roof and wetsuits and packed lunches in our backpacks.

Between Bideford and Wadebridge the coastline is convoluted and difficult, with wooded combes leading to tiny coves, secret beaches down tiny farm tracks and few places to park up the van and look out to sea that aren't busy with holidaymakers on summer days like these. So hiking in is the best way to see it au naturel. Much of the coast is unspoiled by roads and protected by law, and all the more beautiful for it.

The lane is narrow, with grass growing down the middle. We pass a farm, then arrive at an area where it's possible to park a few cars. We are the first to arrive, which means we'll have the beach to ourselves, we hope.

We sling on our backpacks, unload the boards and head off down the green lane that will take us to the gorge we must descend to get to the beach.

I have lived along the Atlantic Highway for over 20 years now, so I've explored much of the coast while searching for good, uncrowded surf. It's easy for me to be blasé about it as I have driven it in snow, rain, hail, thunder and bright spring sunshine. It's home turf. Even so, the butterflies in my stomach flutter every time I set off on days like these. Will we hit the jackpot today? Will all my dreams come true? Will it be the best it's ever been?

The lane is overgrown with dock leaves and grasses between the high banks that are topped with bramble and blackthorn. There are butterflies

and insects buzzing around us, taking flight as we disturb them with our clumsy booted footsteps. We arrive at the river and take a right turn between the spurs of the steep valley, dodging muddy patches where the marsh grass grows tall. We reach the top of the gorge and start to clamber down to the wooden bridge that crosses the river. It's not easy, but we don't mind: it's one of the reasons we'll have the place to ourselves.

Now we can see what the day will bring us. The tide is still high, but the water is blue and translucent, glowing like turquoise. There is a small swell, creating little waves across the reef, each one similar to the last. I strip off, change into my board shorts and dive straight in. It's my first surf of the summer without a wetsuit – it doesn't happen very often – and the water is cold, but only for a moment. The sun warms my bare back as I paddle out. I surf the small waves, thrilled to be here at all, let alone doing my favourite thing on a deserted beach that's no more than five miles from home.

Lizzy swims out through the surf to bob about with me in the water. 'Remember this,' I say to her as she ducks under a wave. I catch a few more and we head in for lunch and to warm up.

As the tide recedes we take to the water again, this time in our wetsuits. The ebb has revealed a strip of sand at low tide. It's perfect, with no footprints other than ours. We paddle out and catch a few waves, then decide to explore the southern half of the beach – the bay is split into two by a promontory of rock which juts out into the waves. We paddle around and beach ourselves on the sand. It's too hot in our suits so we strip off and leave them on a rock to dry. Wearing nothing, we head out into the waves again for a rare chance to surf completely unencumbered by any kind of clothing or bathing suit. We feel like naughty children stealing some fun from under the noses of

our own more sensible selves. Total abandonment makes us giggle as we catch waves in turn, laughing at our nakedness. We're teenagers, living in the now. Nothing else matters. It's lovely – delicious – to feel the salt water on our skin.

Then, the dream is shattered: we see someone climbing over the rocks that screen us from the main beach. They must have arrived while we were in the water. They are not alone: it's a family with two small kids, no doubt looking for the same peace and quiet we seek ourselves. We paddle in to the beach, covering ourselves with our boards as we stroll up the sand to find our drying wetsuits. We duck behind the rock, sitting in a rock pool to work out what to do next. There's a bigger rock a little way away where we might be able to hide and put our suits on, but it'll be a dash. I decide to front it out and walk over in plain sight, covering myself with my board. It's not so easy for Lizzy, who does her best to cover up as she strides across no man's land to the shelter of the big rock.

We dress quickly, still laughing – although it's really difficult to put on a wet wetsuit in a hurry – and paddle back out into the sea. Once we are out in the sea, safely beyond the breaking waves, we look back at the beach, the thrift-covered cliff and the little gorge that brought us here. This is North Cornwall at its best: a paradise down a little lane that you have to make an effort to find. It's the jackpot, and it is worth every trip that doesn't end in such fun and laughter in the sunshine. But today is the day.

'Remember this,' I say to myself as we trudge back up the gorge.

# BODMIN MOOR

## ESCAPE TO THE COUNTRY

Bodmin Moor covers a large area of North Cornwall. Sometimes you don't even know you're in it until you reach those high, barren stretches of common land bordered by a cattle grid and a tumbledown stone wall. This route takes in the best of Bodmin and include tors, lakes, quarries and ancient sites.

BEST FOR:
**A day out on the moor**

START/END:
**Bolventor**

MILEAGE: 25 **miles (40 kilometres)**

DAYS TO EXPLORE: **2**

OS LANDRANGER MAP: **200**

THE SOUTH WEST

**There is a thick sea fog** at the coast. A sea fret. It has come rolling in across the water like a cool, heavy tidal wave, engulfing the cliffs and beaches with its impenetrable depth. We can't see more than 30 yards across the beach, so it's hopeless thinking about a day on the sand. No matter, we have a plan. We drive away from the coast, away from Widemouth Bay, and almost immediately we hit the sunshine.

As we drive south on the A39 the change is immediate: to our right it's foggy and cool, at around 13 degrees centigrade, while to our left the fields are basking in hot sunshine. As we pass the threshold of this coastal obscurity the temperature gauge on the car climbs steadily to 23 degrees.

The further inland we go the hotter it gets, and when we arrive at Minions it's 25 degrees, even though it's still only early May and three o'clock in the afternoon. We drive through the village and park in a small but busy car park adjoining the open ground that slopes away up to the Cheesewring, a granite tor consisting of a pile of slabs, sitting above a disused quarry. We walk out on to the moor, towards the Hurlers, a group

of three stone circles, and the Pipers, a pair of standing stones. There are several wild ponies with newborn foals basking in the sun as we pass. As semi-feral animals often left here to take advantage of grazing rights dating back to medieval times, they are not used to human interaction so they cannot be approached, but Maggie and Charlie are intrigued.

The moor we walk across is open, green and largely flat, except for what look like a few deep ditches that we assume are the remains of mine workings. We are slap-bang in the middle of the Cornish Mining World Heritage site on Bodmin Moor, so it stands to reason that parts of the landscape here would have been shaped by man. Behind us Caradon Hill rises like a dome to 371m (1,217ft), while ahead of us the Cheeswring stands tall atop a granite cliff turned from hillock to bluff by quarrying. We reach a fork in the track and Lizzy guides us to the left, on the smaller of the two paths, towards another hillock topped by large pieces of granite. The ground gently slopes away from us in a crucible-like valley. There are farm buildings at the bottom, and stone walls marking out pens and fields.

As we get closer I see that there are a couple of promontories sticking out into the valley, made from piles of rock. With them on our right we come to the apex of the rise and arrive at the quarry. It's so well hidden in the hillside that you'd never know it was here unless you were guided to it or stumbled upon it. We stand at the top of a 5m (16.5ft) drop looking down at a still body of water, a disused quarry. On three sides the walls are vertical, between 2 and 7 or 8m (6.5 to 23–26ft) tall, while on the fourth side the banks drop down to form a rocky beach made up of huge slabs of granite. The water is clear and deep, as we can see the bottom only at the places where the rocks are less than about 3m (10ft) deep.

We change into our wetsuits and walk around to the lowest of the drops, a height of about 3m (10ft). I run from the top and launch myself into the abyss. I clear the quarry wall and feel like I am floating for a moment before gravity pulls me into the water. It's cold, and when I open my eyes underwater, I see it's clear. I see bubbles and my feet for a moment before I resurface. Maggie and Charlie, seeing it's safe, clamber to the edge and launch themselves off too, holding their noses as they go. Next it's Liz's turn. She surfaces and soon we are all floating in the water, smiling, looking up at the blue sky.

We survey the walls around us. Which one next?

We swim for the beach to start again...

# THE DRIVING

Bodmin Moor is wonderful for aimless campervan wandering, with a good map. And if you want to see some of the best of it, this route, a W-shaped, 'circular' drive, will show you.

You can do it any way round you wish; if you're heading west on the A30, it's easy to take the first turn off past the Jamaica Inn at Bolventor, which is signposted to Colliford Lake. Slow down as you approach the turn-off to the Smugglers Museum and then take the next turn-off at the top of the hill, following the brown sign. Immediately you're in the wildest part of Bodmin Moor, where unkempt softwood plantations shelter ramshackle homesteads, and moss-covered walls do their best to contain shaggy-coated ponies, Belted Galloway cattle and hardy sheep. It's a single track which follows the reservoir round its western shore. There are stopping

points along the road for a cuppa or a picnic, with lovely lakeside views.

At Colliford Downs there is a small crossroads. You have a choice here: take a right and you'll head to St Neot and towards Cardinham Woods and Lanhydrock House if you want to stray off our map. Take the left and you'll follow the eastern shore of the reservoir back up to Jamaica Inn. It's a rambling, narrow, wild and open road through stark moorland and wild farming country. Don't stray from the path, lads! The road will take you back to the tiny hamlet of Bolventor and the tourist trap of the Smugglers Museum.

At the Jamaica Inn, take a right and then immediately turn right again on to the tiny road that follows the young River Fowey. This is a delightful road, following the river along the western bank for a few glorious, sheltered miles all the way down to Golitha Falls. The landscape is softer here, more secluded, with willow and beech. Signposts promise the chance of seeing otters.

**Nearest van hire**

**O'Connors Campers**
- www.oconnorscampers.co.uk

A stop-off at Golitha Falls, at the end of this stretch of road over a little stone bridge, is highly recommended. It's popular because it's so beautiful; the walk will take you an hour or so through ancient beech and oak woods. Turning left after the Golitha Falls stop will take you on the unclassified road towards Minions and the turn-off to Siblyback Lake. Entering Minions, park on the left for the Cheesewring, stone circle and quarries. In the village there are tea shops and a pub. As you leave the village, take the first left past the engine houses: this will take you down an extraordinary road with beautiful views over the Tamar Valley and into Henwood, a fabulous village with narrow streets (that's a warning for the big units), and bring you out on to the B3254 – another nice road which, if you turn left at Congdon's Shop on to the B3257, will lead you quickly back to the A30; take the first left to return to Bolventor. (Continuing straight on after Congdon's Shop will take you to Launceston.)

## PLACES TO STAY

**Colliford Tavern**
Colliford Lake, Nr St Neot, Liskeard, Cornwall, PL14 6PZ
**tel:** 01208 821335
**web:** www.colliford.com
**email:** info@colliford.com

**info:** *A small campsite overlooking Colliford Lake in a secluded spot. Pub next door. Sadly, no lake access.*

**Cheesewring Farm**
Minions, Liskeard, Cornwall, PL14 5LJ
**tel:** 01579 362200/07836 294296
**web:** www.cheesewringfarm.co.uk
**email:** info@cheesewringfarm.co.uk

**info:** *A Certificated Location site with limited pitches in a fantastic location below the Cheesewring and with amazing views over the moor.*

**Siblyback Lake Camping**
Siblyback Lake Watersports Centre, Nr Liskeard, Cornwall, PL14 6ER
**tel:** 01579 346522
**web:** www.southwestlakes.co.uk/camping/siblyback-lake

**info:** *One of the South West Lakes Trust's lovely lakeside campsites. Pitches on the water with watersports, café and walking/cycling trails nearby. A great find and much underrated.*

# IN THE AREA

**Minions, World Heritage Site**  A fascinating area where the wild moor meets industrialisation. Engine houses and quarries sit side by side with the Cheesewring and the Hurlers standing stones. Plus wild swimming.
• www.cornwalls.co.uk/minions

**Cardinham Woods**  Try your wheels on the Beast of Bodmin, an excellent mountain bike trail, or just walk about in the woods admiring nature in this beautiful forest. Café, too.  • www.forestryengland.uk/cardinham-woods

**Bodmin Jail**  The scariest, most haunted building in all of Cornwall. Hardly surprising since it has been the site of many a hanging. Tragic stories. Scary stuff.  • www.bodminjail.org

**Lanhydrock House**  A National Trust-owned Victorian mansion with gardens, walking tails and forest. See life above and below stairs. Plus some fantastic free cycle trails and a great pump track.  • www.nationaltrust.org.uk/lanhydrock

**Golitha Falls**  A beautiful woodland consisting of beech and native oak, plus the tumbling, gurgling and young River Fowey tumbling through it. Mossy boulders, old mine shafts, tangled roots and an otherworldly feel. Great place for a walk or a paddle.  • www.woodlandtrust.org.uk/visiting-woods/wood/27756/golitha-falls

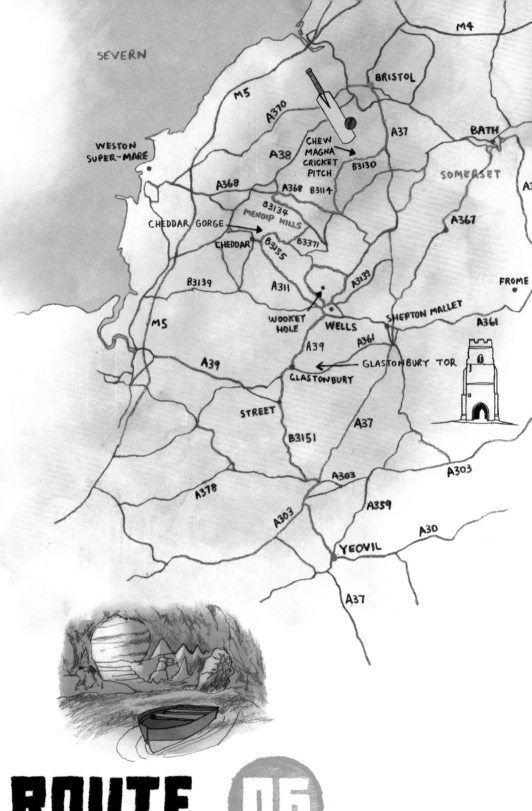

SEVERN

M4

BRISTOL

M5

A370

BATH

WESTON
SUPER-MARE

CHEW
MAGNA
CRICKET
PITCH

A37

B3130

SOMERSET

A38

A368

A368   B3114

B3134

A367

MENDIP HILLS

CHEDDAR GORGE

B3135

B3371

FROME

CHEDDAR

B3139

A311

A3139

M5

WOOKEY
HOLE

SHEPTON MALLET

A361

WELLS

A39

A361

GLASTONBURY TOR

A39

GLASTONBURY

STREET

A37

B3151

A303

A303

A378

A359

A303

A30

YEOVIL

A37

# ROUTE 06

# BRISTOL TO YEOVIL

## THE HIPPY TRAIL

Between Bristol and Yeovil lies a version of England that no one should miss, with ducks and cricket pitches, churches, mills and even the nearest thing we have to an Alpine gorge. Along the way you might come across some tourist tat, a show cave, an ancient site and some hippy paraphernalia, but always at the heart of it is England, with its elasticated waistbands strolling around ancient sites and its patterned silks searching for some kind of spiritual truth – as well as its miles and miles of beautiful country roads, some with views, some with tall hedges bursting with colour and others with stalls selling strawberries and cream. Stop and take it all in.

BEST FOR:
**Meandering in the Mendips**

START: **Bristol**

END: **Yeovil**

MILEAGE: **65 miles (105 kilometres)**

DAYS TO EXPLORE: **2**

OS LANDRANGER MAP: **172, 183**

THE SOUTH WEST

85

By the time I get the van parked in Glastonbury I am not feeling very spiritual at all. But I guess, in a town that appears to be looking to its past for divine inspiration, I am part of the modern-day car-parking problem in my camper. Parking is a bit of a headache, especially since the signs to the Glastonbury Tor park and ride peter out somewhere along the A361. Still, in trying to find somewhere to leave the van, I've had a good look at the town.

The van's a little big for the tiny, car-sized spaces in the abbey car park, and there's no hope of slotting into any of the on-street parking places. I'm on my third circuit, but I am absolutely determined to take in the Tor and the vibes of this magical, mystical place, so I persevere. I turn left at the top of High Street and find my way into the Butt Close car park. There, behind an old converted Luton lorry with a stovepipe poking out of the roof, is a van-sized space. I pull in and lock up.

I duck through a little alleyway and come out on to Glastonbury's colourful high street. It's not like any other high street I've ever been on. There's no H&M or Primark, very little evidence of a chain-store invasion and barely a Greggs or Costa in sight. It's more Khao San Road than Kilburn High Road, but without the lights and the fuss. There are more mullets and dreads, Thai fisherman pants and rainbow jumpers here than anywhere I've been in a while. And with shop names like Man, Myth and Magik selling 'finely crafted items to aid your spiritual journey' it's easy to slide straight into stereotyping and cliché. But hey, these are my people more than the football-shirted hoons I come across everywhere else, so I give it time to settle in my consciousness.

As a surfer, van dweller (albeit part time) and former longhair I feel at

home here, although I'm not sure I'd ever find myself going as far as popping in to The Cat and The Cauldron for some 1990s raver threads. But even so, it's refreshing, whatever your belief system, to see independents thriving and big business staying (or being kept) away, even though what remains might be quite far along the road to New Age enlightenment.

But why not? Glastonbury is a deeply spiritual place, despite the parking issues. It is the site of one of England's oldest Saxon churches, at Glastonbury Abbey, where it is also believed King Arthur is buried. Glastonbury is the Isle of Avalon and, if you believe the legends, was visited by Joseph of Arimathea. Did those feet in ancient time walk upon England's mountain green? Maybe. Or maybe not. But whatever it is you believe, there is no doubt that there is something about this small town in Somerset that separates it from its neighbours. Like finds like and settles, in order to find another way.

I take a turn to the left and walk along the main road, following directions carved into an old stone water fountain that's long since dried up by the look of it. Taking a left into an estate of houses, I head uphill, past

the ashram (it had to be) and into the fields at the back of the houses. I cross a field, leap over a stile and then come out on a quiet lane with overgrown hedges. Elderflowers and cow parsley make up the colour, along with pink campions and buttercups among the tall and seeded grasses. I pass a man with dreadlocks, stripped to the waist and barefoot, wearing harem pants and with a guitar slung over his shoulder. I look him in the eye and smile. He sees right through me and strolls off down the road towards town. I guess, without my curls, I am just another straight-edged visitor.

I pass a pair of grey-haired ladies taking pictures of themselves ('I think I've got it set to selfie') when I suspect they actually wanted a picture of the church tower on top of the Tor.

I go through a gate and am on the route to the Tor, a concrete pathway with steps leading up the steep north-eastern side. I try not to look at the view as I climb, saving it for the final moments of my ascent, which come a lot quicker than I had thought. There are a few people sitting and chatting, some taking pictures, a couple smooching in the grass. Sheep graze on the lower slopes.

I stop and look, for the first time. If Somerset was a sea, then Glastonbury Tor would surely be its greatest island, a beacon among the levels that surround it. The view is wonderful. To the north I can see the Mendips, from where I have just come, to the north-west the Bristol Channel and to the south the Blackdown Hills. Below me the poplars and field systems of Somerset really do look like a patchwork quilt in all the hues of green. Sun glints off windows and solar panels in Street and Glastonbury below me. It is really quite peaceful. There are no cars, no shops and no hassle, just a remarkable island of colour and spirituality, swimming in a sea of countryside. A refuge from the banality of Middle England and its Costas and Primarks and the vapid and useless trappings of modern life. It's all right here, I think. I get it now.

Glastonbury is a very special place. I think I'll stay for a bit.

I wonder if I put enough money in the meter.

# THE DRIVING

Leaving Bristol on the A37, it's surprising how quickly the suburbs change into open country and the traffic subsides. At the first glimpse of the open country beyond Bristol's hills, you'll need to take a right turn, along the B3130 towards Chew Magna down a narrow lane with tall, banked sides and then out into open country before arriving at Chew Magna. This is your first glimpse of England as it should be, with cricket pitch, tall trees, grand houses and creamy-coloured houses crowded around narrow streets. Everything is right with Chew Magna. It has local shops, people busily buzzing around and an air of Midsomer about it.

Leave the village on the B3114, a right turn at the Sacred Heart Catholic Church, and head towards West Harptree, pausing only to follow the signs to Chew Valley Lake, a lovely man-made reservoir with café and picnic areas, and a lot of ducks who are after your bread. At West Harptree take the right-hand turn and follow the A368 towards Blagdon. This is a glorious road at the foot of the north side of the Mendips. It weaves its way between the hills and the flatlands, through tiny villages and past beautiful mature trees, copper beeches and chestnuts. Rickford Chapel is a delightful spot: keep your foot off the gas and enjoy it as you dawdle past. At Burrington take a left turn on to the B3134 and head up into the Mendips via Burrington Combe. You'll pass Goatchurch Cavern, a 750m (2,460ft) cavern, and rock faces on the left-hand side as you drive up into the shallow birch-, hazel-

and blackthorn-filled gorge. After driving a couple of miles along the open top of the hills, take a right-hand turn on the B3371 towards Cheddar. After making another right turn, you will be at the top of the gorge, where a series of tight, steep bends will bring you down Cliff Road and into Cheddar via the magnificent limestone cleft. There are places to park up as you descend, with a proliferation of car parks appearing the closer you get to the show caves and village. Stop here if you like touristy stuff (there is a lot of it); otherwise, take a left on to the A371 towards Wells.

I took a detour to Wookey Hole, another famous show cave, but couldn't bring myself to go in there again as it reminded me of wet days when I was a kid and we'd been camping at Minehead. However, taking the turn-off pays off as it means you can get out via Ebbor Gorge, a very narrow road that takes you to the top of Ebbor Gorge National Nature Reserve, past the Deerleap Standing Stones and past one of the very finest views in the Mendips.

At Priddy take right-hand turn to get back on track and pick up the A39, the Old Bristol Road, into Wells. After a few wiggles and lights at Wells, the A39 will take you to the jewel in the crown of this wonderful relaxed drive – Glastonbury and the Tor – before you pick up the lovely B3151 that will take you on to Yeovil and the A303, your escape lane back to London, or, in the other direction, the road that will take you on to the A30 and the West.

### Nearest van hire

**Moovans Campervan Rentals**
• www.moovans.com

## PLACES TO STAY

**Ebborways Farm Campsite**
Ebborways Farm, Pelting Road, Priddy, Wells, Somerset, BA5 3BA
**web:** www.ebborwaysfarm.co.uk
**email:** chriskdyke@gmail.com
**tel:** 01749 676339

**info:** *Just a field, some compost toilets and a tap. Winner!*

**Old Oaks Camping, Glastonbury**
Wick, Glastonbury, Somerset, BA6 8JS
**web:** www.theoldoaks.co.uk
**email:** info@theoldoaks.co.uk
**tel:** 01458 831437

**info:** *Adults-only camping for people who don't like kids. Nice site, but no kids.*

**Dragon Willows Farm**
Godney Road, Glastonbury, Somerset, BA6 9AF
**web:** www.dragonwillowsfarm.co.uk
**email:** info@dragonwillowsfarm.co.uk
**tel:** 07785 985643

**info:** *Eco-friendly, green-minded farm camping in Glastonbury with nowt but somewhere to empty your tanks and stock up on water.*

# IN THE AREA

**Glastonbury Abbey**  The final resting place of King Arthur, the place Joseph of Arimathea came to, the site of the earliest church, place of fascination for centuries, home of the Holy Thorn and 36 acres of sanctuary in the heart of Glastonbury.  • www.glastonburyabbey.com

**Cheddar Gorge and Caves**  It's 122m (400ft) deep and 4.8km (3 miles) long. But it's not full of cheese! Adventures, caving, climbing and all kinds of stuff at one of the UK's best-known show caves.  • www.cheddargorge.co.uk

**Wookey Hole**  Scary cave diving, fun and cheesy frolics at the UK's biggest cave system. And this one *is* full of cheese.  • www.wookey.co.uk

**Wells Cathedral**  England's smallest city is home to its prettiest cathedral, a Gothic beauty on a Stone Age site.  • www.wellscathedral.org.uk

**Clarks Village, Wells**  From the sublime to the ridiculous. If you don't want to shop on Glasto High Street, then head to the cathedral of vacuous purchasing at this designer outlet village, if you like that kind of thing. Probably very disappointing, and may leave you feeling empty.
• www.clarksvillage.co.uk

# ROUTE 07

# THE RIVER DART

## FROM THE MOOR TO THE SEA

This route takes in some of the very best of South Devon and Dartmoor. Ever varying, it'll give you a taste of the wildness of the moor, whose rivers eventually crash, gush and meander down to the contrasting peace and tranquillity of the south coast. Expect to see huge views and stunning vistas, beautiful villages and lively, independent-minded towns.

BEST FOR:
**Wild places, walks and swims**

START:
**Tavistock**

END:
**Blackpool Sands**

MILEAGE: **45 miles (73 kilometres)**

DAYS TO EXPLORE: **2**

OS LANDRANGER MAP: **191, 202**

THE SOUTH WEST

**Wistman's Wood** has long been a place of mystery and wonder, legend and fear. Ever since I first read about it in Christopher Somerville's *Britain and Ireland's Best Wild Places*, I have wanted to go there and see it for myself. I have read much elsewhere, too, about this ancient, stunted forest near the source of the West Dart River. Supposedly one of Devon's most haunted places, where adders creep from beneath every rock and which no one dares to enter at night, it's where ancient druids held their pagan rituals. A procession of mourners is rumoured to pass here at night, accompanied by the howl of a dog, a scampering, ghostly Jack Russell killed by the snakes. People love a good mystery, don't they?

It's a bright day at the end of August when Liz and I park up at Two Bridges and pull on our walking boots. We've got no OS map with us, so we bicker a little about whether we are ready to follow this route, and about whether we are fully prepared in general, as we find the well-worn path, slip through the gate and set out across the moor. Really, there's no need for a map at all as the route is clear and the path easy to follow.

We pass a cottage en route, in a little dell by the side of the river, which is nothing more than a wide stream at this stage in its development. At the side of the house is a mossy hollow, out of which grows a solitary mountain ash. Its branches are heavy with deep orange berries, a fiery contrast to the bright yellow of the gorse that's in flower on the moor behind it.

After the cottage, we walk on to the moor proper, and the path, dotted with smooth granite boulders, becomes soft and peaty. It's open and wild, heavily grazed down to tufty clumps of grass and reed, gorse and fern. We see the wood ahead of us, a shade darker than the rest of the moorland, almost lost in the vastness of the landscape. The dwarf oaks are no more than 4.5 metres (15ft) high and form an oval clump on the west-facing slope. We enter the forest and immediately can see why it's long been feared and revered. Big mossy boulders make walking (and probably also grazing) difficult. The low, twisted, intertwining oaks are dripping with lichens and mosses. We make our way into the centre of the wood carefully. Liz asks me if I'm worried about snakes, to which I reply that I wasn't – up until then, I had forgotten about the legends. But I'm OK, although I raise my voice slightly as we walk. Between the boulders I notice bright green wood sorrel and all kinds of fungi. There are supposed to be over a hundred types of lichen growing here, but I can identify none of them – I wish I could. But I can still enjoy the earthy smell of the woods, the beauty of the ancient oaks and the carpet of mossy boulders. It's an ancient, soulful landscape, but I feel no fear. We wander down the hillside to sit by the river and talk about the rest of our journey. Liz sits on a rock and dangles her feet in

the clear, peaty water. It's all the planning we'll do on this trip, but no matter. We will follow the river from here, just below the watershed at Beardown Tors, to the sea.

When we do reach the sea, beyond Dartmouth, we drive along the top of the cliffs on the way to Blackpool Sands, our intended finish point. We miss the turn-off to the beach and are forced, by the traffic and the size of the van, to continue on to turn around. We climb away from the Scots pines and laurels that inhabit the sheltered valley behind Blackpool Sands. We pass a steep-sided valley leading to a sliver of sand and a slice of beautifully calm sea beyond. There's a lay-by not far away with space enough for the van and a stile that looks like it could lead us down a tiny zigzagging path a little further along, so we abandon the plan to swim at Blackpool Sands and make a new one instead. We park, hop over the stile and make our way carefully down the valley side to the beach. Before long we are taking our boots off, shedding our clothes and running into the sea with giddy abandon.

We've covered only around 50 miles since Wistman's Wood, but it feels like we are worlds away. From the dark, beautiful wood high on the moor we've ended up here, at a secret slice of heaven – a beach with brightly coloured shingles, caves and no one to tut or tsk at us as we dry off our bare bodies in the last patch of sun.

Later, on our way back up the river, when the sun turns blood red and drops into the clear space between dark clouds and the moor, we pass the turn-off to Wistman's Wood. Briefly I think of following our footsteps back into the forest of twisted oaks and dark mysteries, but it's just a fleeting thought. Instead, we chase the sunset between the tors until the moor turns black.

As the darkness descends we're glad we're in the van before the ghostly procession begins.

# THE DRIVING

**WARNING:** Not suitable for units over 2.28m (7'6") wide.

Devon is lovely. Devon is popular. Devon is, for many, a heaven on earth. But for the slow-road traveller it's not always as perfect as you might imagine it to be. There is a very good reason for this, and it's to do with the way Devon's roads have developed over the years. As is the case for much of England, the roads have grown up from green lanes and bridleways. Little of the road network has been planned, but instead has been built out of nothing, even the A30 and A38, which are the county's main routes. These lanes and byways have traditionally been bounded by a feature known as the 'Devon Bank'. These tall earth and stone banks topped with trees were originally designed to contain livestock. Some of them are hundreds of years old. Today, due to the decline in coppicing the (often hazel) trees that grow on the top of these banks, the banks can grow out of control, creating an impressive physical barrier between you, the road user, and the countryside. In short, this means there's not much to see. It can be

disorientating and claustrophobic, which is frustrating when it really should feel sunny and open.

The way to get around this is to head for open moorland, common grazing land or the coast. And that's, in part, what this route is about. Start at Tavistock, an ancient market and stannary town whose most famous son is Sir Francis Drake. Take the B3357 out of town and head up towards Dartmoor. You'll pass through an excellent example of these forgotten hazel-topped banks almost as soon as you turn off. It's grown to such an extent here that the trees form a tunnel of bright green over the curving road. Leaving the safety of the trees, you'll head up on to open moorland on the beautifully named Pork Hill. There's a viewpoint here. Do stop and take it all in. From the top of Pork Hill it's open country for a while. You'll see the granite tors, farmhouses, old quarries, ancient sites and even Dartmoor

Prison as you continue to Two Bridges (the stop for Wistman's Wood). This route follows the B3351 from here (signposted Ashburton), but take the time to follow the B3212 for a few miles to Postbridge, where you can see the very fine clapper bridge, meet the abrupt man who works in the post office and enjoy a picnic by the side of the West Dart.

After Dartmeet you'll begin the descent into Ashburton. This is a roller coaster, and it takes some nerve! It's got a couple of steep (20% and 25%) sections and you may meet the odd cow on the road (we did); there are also two narrow bridges, at Holne Bridge and New Bridge. For wild swimmers, the West Dart upstream from New Bridge is a bit of a Mecca, where you'll find Sharrah Pool and other enticing swimming spots.

At Ashburton you'll need to hit the Devon Expressway, the A38, heading west towards Plymouth, for the turn-off to Totnes, the A384. This winding road follows the Dart into the town, which sits at the furthest tidal reach of the river. It's a fiercely independent town with a reputation for alternative living. It's beautiful too, a real gem in the hilly Devonian landscape. As is

usual in Devon, it's hard to get a measure of the place because of the geography.

The A381 will take you to Halwell, where you'll need to pick up the A3122 to Dartmouth. If you ever wanted a taste of Devon's road system, this will give you it. The road meanders across the hinterland behind and above the Dart estuary, and it's not until you drop down the steep hill into Dartmouth that you get a feel for what you've been skirting. But oh, is it worth the drive! Seeing the estuary for the first time is a joy. With the coloured terraces of houses opposite in Kingswear and the yachts bobbing away at their moorings, it's a real wow place to end up. The B3205 will take you along the seafront and back out to the A379 to Blackpool Sands, but do meander and wander a while. Dartmouth has two river crossings which will take you to Kingswear and Brixham, lots of shops and a really lovely feel.

## PLACES TO STAY

### Tavistock Camping and Caravanning Club Site

Higher Longford, Moorshop, Tavistock, Devon, PL19 9LQ

**web:** www.campingandcaravanningclub.co.uk

**tel:** 01822 618672

**info:** *Well situated for the beginning of this route and for access to Dartmoor via the B3357.*

---

### Leonards Cove Holiday Park

Dartmouth, Devon, TQ6 0NR

**web:** www.leonardscove.co.uk

**email:** info@leonardscove.co.uk

**tel:** 01803 770206

**info:** *A nicely situated holiday park with camping and touring pitches just outside Blackpool Sands beach. Sea views and nice bar and restaurant on site.*

---

### Steamer Quay Caravan and Motorhome Club Site

Steamer Quay Road, Totnes, Devon, TQ9 5AL

**web:** www.caravanclub.co.uk

**tel:** 01803 862738

**info:** *Standard C and M Club Site in a rural location and yet close enough to Totnes to walk into town.*

---

### River Dart Country Park and Campsite

River Dart Country Park, Ashburton, Devon, TQ13 7NP

**web:** www.riverdart.co.uk

**email:** info@riverdart.co.uk

**tel:** 01364 652511

**info:** *A family-friendly campsite and holiday park with loads of activities for the kids and plenty to do for the grown-ups too. Right on the river.*

# IN THE AREA

**Bellever Forest, Princetown, Dartmoor**  A National Park forest on the banks of the Dart with lots to explore and walking routes that will take you to Postbridge clapper bridge. A great place for a picnic.

**Dartington Hall**  A social experiment gone right, with the lovely Barn Cinema, cultural events, shops, food and drink and generally lovely vibe.
• www.dartington.org

**Dartmouth Castle**  Brilliantly situated, quite old and used a lot over the centuries. A boat ride from Dartmouth, with walks, cream teas, the lot.  • www.english-heritage.org.uk/visit/places/dartmouth-castle

**South Devon Railway**  For the steam enthusiasts, old rolling stock, in the form of steam locomotives, on seven miles of a former branch line, and the possibility of a Devon cream tea (with the cream on first, goddammit).
• www.southdevonrailway.co.uk

### Nearest van hire

**coast2coast Camper Hire**
• www.coast2coastcamperhire.co.uk

# THE SOUTH AND SOUTH EAST

While you might not think it's got
much to offer apart from commuters and stockbroker
belts, the South East of England gave me some true delights.
I drove the length of the Thames from Dartford to Abingdon and loved
it, not only for its beauty but also for its history, culture and the difference
between skyscraper and quietly flowing river. It was a marvel. Equally,
the south coast, from Worthing to Beachy Head, offers a suburban sprawl
of beautiful beaches, promenades and south coast vernacular, including
elegant Regency squares and art deco pavilions. And beach huts. Lots of
beach huts. Head inland from here and you'll encounter the A272,
England's most English of cross-country routes. Tally ho!

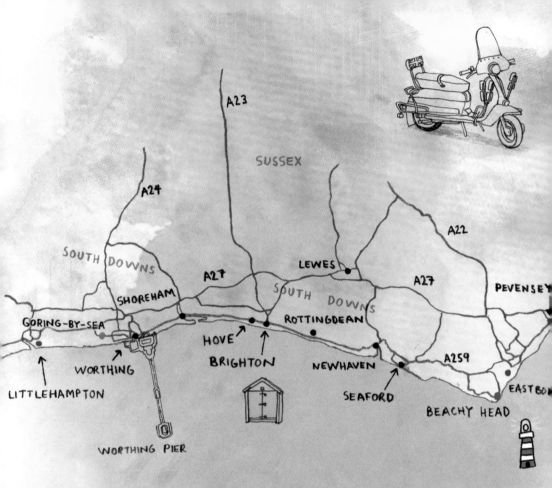

A23

SUSSEX

A24

SOUTH DOWNS

A27

LEWES

A22

SOUTH DOWNS

A27

PEVENSEY

SHOREHAM

GORING-BY-SEA

ROTTINGDEAN

HOVE

BRIGHTON

NEWHAVEN

A259

WORTHING

LITTLEHAMPTON

SEAFORD

EASTBO

BEACHY HEAD

WORTHING PIER

ENGLISH CHANNEL

# ROUTE 08

# SOUTH COAST SPRAWL

## A CRUISE ALONG THE PROM

Wind down the window and crank up the tunes. There are 20 miles of low-speed people-watching, architecture-admiring, ice-cream-eating, kiss-me-quick wanderings to be had on Sussex's south coast. From Goring in the west to Peacehaven in the east, the A259 crawls along the south coast's urban sprawl at a snail's pace, offering the ultimate in slow road cruising. And all of it's just yards from the beach. Lovely jubbly.

BEST FOR:
**Cruising along the prom**

START:
**Goring-by-Sea**

END: **Beachy Head**

MILEAGE: **34 miles (54 kilometres)**

DAYS TO EXPLORE: **2**

OS LANDRANGER MAP: **198, 199**

THE SOUTH AND SOUTH EAST

III

I am surprised to hit the coast just like that, at a little roundabout at the end of a row of suburban 1930s houses that face off against a field of wheat that could just as easily be in Pinner. I've been looking for the sea among the sprawl and finally I hit it at Goring-by-Sea, down Sea Lane. Go figure. This is the first point at which I've been able to access the coast because to the west, at Angmering, the valuable coastal strip is taken up with mean-spirited private estates, which is all very well if you live in them but not so good for the slow road traveller.

I take a left, past a beacon of a house that looks to be half leisure centre and half art deco landmark, complete with round turrets and glass balconies, that probably costs a packet to live in and was probably developed in the noughties. Then there's a field, Goring Gap. For a moment I'm on a coastal breeze, with the sea to my right and open fields to my left. But no, hang on, I hit houses very quickly and I'm back in suburbia again.

I carry on, heading east towards Worthing. There are mansions on the landward side of me, with manicured lawns behind low brick walls. Occasionally there is a new build of silvered wood and render, solar and glass, all straight lines and angles between the tidy examples of middle England 1930s vernacular.

A little further on, when the beach huts begin on the seaward side, the houses get a little smaller, but still seem to belong to another place. It's suburbia on sea and it seems alien to me. I'm used to crashing waves and small, squat farmhouses sheltering in hollows from the prevailing winds.

But here on the south coast it's much more benign. No wonder Sussex is the second most popular place to resettle after retirement for Brits.

As I move down the coast the architecture changes again. Worthing has a few ugly 1960s high-rises and more brick-and-tiled mansions, but it soon changes – to my relief – to rendered columned Georgian and Victorian terraces, with elegant wrought-iron balconies and balustrades. But these are countered by a Premier Inn, a newly built apartment block and the odd art deco newcomer. Still, on the whole it's elegant and tidy and a pleasure to see the Victorian beach shelters and beach huts give it a jolly, good-natured air.

In Onslow Court in Worthing I see a reflection of exciting times that didn't quite get the upgrade it needed. It's a magnificent curved-fronted 1930s building, with ironwork dripping rust stains down its unloved paintwork that makes it look like a liner in dry dock awaiting a refit.

Moving on, I pass more rows of suburban drivel, unremarkable brick-built apartment blocks and even a giant concrete car park, until the A259 hits the River Adur at Shoreham-by-Sea and Shoreham Port. I take a diversion into the maze of streets leading up to Shoreham Redoubt. The houses are smaller here, with many looking unloved, but just as many having had a cherry seaside makeover with glass and concrete boarding. Some plots have been razed and built again in ultra-modern seaside style: more glass, more weatherboarding, more silvered wood cladding. Outside houses there are boats, dinghies, kayaks and canoes, all waiting for the right day to hit the water again. Some, though, I fear, never will.

Then I'm into Hove and Brighton, with the mix of the cream-coloured Regency terraces and squares, the pier, tall hotels and modern blocks sitting side by side with the Victorian ironwork. It's all rather lovely, and I enjoy every traffic light and halt in the flow to be able to look at and examine the architecture of the south coast. It's remarkable. When I have been here before I have been impatient. Today it's all about lingering. The sad and skeletal remains of the West Pier contrast with the brash colour of the Palace Pier: it seems impossible that the former should still be there at all in such a state.

A worthy detour takes in the Madeira Drive Arches, an ongoing project below the level of the road where you can park up next to the beach and grab a coffee from a café. I expect to see mods and rockers fighting it out there (it is Easter Bank Holiday, after all), but maybe it's a bit early in the season.

Beyond Brighton, and after the open spaces behind its marina, we go for a lower-rent option: smaller houses, less trendy shops, and less opulence and wealth are apparent in Saltdean, Rottingdean, Peacehaven and Newhaven. And then I pass through Seaford, a mix of flinted churches, Victorian houses and 1970s development. It's the last of the south coast sprawl before the A259 rises up on to the Downs towards Beachy Head and the Seven Sisters, those crumbling, symbolic white cliffs that define our nation like nothing else. At the top I dare to look over the edge, down below to the brown sea and the wind-chopped waves. Next stop France.

# THE DRIVING

This south coast route is about as easy to follow as it's possible to get. It's more about taking it easy and taking it all in than about getting anywhere. Enjoy the sprawl. Watch the people. Crawl at your leisure. Stop and buy an ice cream. Play games on the pier. Start in Ferring, where the coast road is simply called Marine Drive, and then continues eastward until it becomes the A259, passing through Goring, Worthing, Lancing, Shoreham, Hove and Brighton. The only detour you need to take is the road to Birling Gap when you get to East Dean, which is east of Seaford, above the Seven Sisters. That will take you in a loop via Beachy Head and the B2103, so from there you can either make your way down to Eastbourne or back the way you came.

## PLACES TO STAY

**Northbrook Farm Caravan Club Site**
Titnore Way, Worthing, West Sussex, BN13 3RT
**web:** www.caravanclub.co.uk
**tel:** 01903 502962

**info:** *A no-frills site that's a good option as a base for exploring Worthing. No loo block so bring your own loo.*

**Brighton Caravan Club Site**
East Brighton Park, Brighton,
East Sussex, BN2 5TS
**web:** www.caravanclub.co.uk
**tel:** 01273 626546

**info:** *All the usual – good facilities, friendly wardens. Rules and regs.*

Nearest van hire

**CamperVanTastic Ltd**
• www.campervantastic.com

## IN THE AREA

There is a lot to do in Brighton and the surrounding area – too much to mention here. That makes this route one to do slowly. Stop off and enjoy the views, take time for an ice cream and soak up the south coast sprawl!

**Hove Lagoon**  An impressive watersports centre at the west end of Shoreham Harbour offering cable tows for wakeboarding, as well as paddleboarding, sailing and powerboating.  • **www.lagoon.co.uk**

**Brighton Pier**  A theme park on the water with rides, slot machines and shows. Classic seaside entertainment.  • **www.brightonpier.co.uk**

**Arundel Castle**  A lovely castle in a lovely little town. Pretty and worth a stop.  • **www.arundelcastle.org**

**Beachy Head**  There's more to Beachy Head than a big cliff. There's lots to do in the area – and some of the best walking near Brighton.  • **www.beachyhead.org.uk**

# 09

# DARTFORD TO ABINGDON

## WANDERING UPSTREAM

A route that takes in the biggest city in the UK, some of the world's most well-loved monuments, and towns and villages that are about as English as it gets. Plus, you really couldn't do anything other than meander, even if you tried, as you follow the course of England's greatest river on its winding, lazy course upstream from the Dartford Crossing.

BEST FOR: **River views, and everything else!**

START: **Dartford**

END: **Abingdon**

MILEAGE: **121 miles (194 kilometres)**

DAYS TO EXPLORE: **3**

OS LANDRANGER MAP: **164, 174, 175, 176, 177**

THE SOUTH AND SOUTH EAST

121

I am sitting in rush-hour traffic wondering why I have come here to drive the course of the Thames. It's hot and airless and the traffic is moving slowly, barely at all, in fact. Heading headlong into England's worst traffic seems like folly. At least it'll be a slow road, I think to myself.

I approached London from the east, coming up the M25 as far as junction 1A, just before the multi-arched and enormous Dartford Crossing bridge, and diverting left on to the A206 towards the Woolwich Ferry and central London. My idea of following the course of the Thames, as close to the river as I could get, isn't working very well so far, as all I can see are buildings and sky. But then, what did I expect? Some kind of Elysian fantasy of the mighty River Thames, complete with waterside cafés, wildflower meadows and polished wooden-hulled speedboats? That will have to wait.

I sit, window down, arm on the sill, in my VW Crafter, looking at the isolated estates between patches of half-redeveloped post-industrial wasteland, looking and feeling like just another delivery guy making the most of a bad lot on a Wednesday morning.

Happily, the feeling soon goes. I enter Greenwich and I pass the National Maritime Museum and Greenwich Park. In doing so, I realise I have crossed the prime meridian, at zero degrees, the dividing line between the eastern and western hemispheres. To my left, on the hill above me, is Wren's Royal Observatory, the place, if you like, where time begins. Well, Greenwich Mean Time anyway. It's the clock by which the world sets its watch. The palace is where Henry VIII's daughters Mary and Elizabeth were born. It's the heart of the British Empire, the centre of the celestial world, the core of England, if that's what is important about our country. History was made here.

I think of Henry, trotting up the hill to visit his mistresses, of Wren, with vast scrolls of paper, of what this spot means to England and my journeys around it. Then the lights change and I must move on, upstream and into the heart of the city. I realise that, of course, this journey is an essential part of understanding England, then and now.

From the old to the new I go, catching sight of the Shard as I pass by railway arches where busy mechanics work on a collection of classic Porsches. Then I am crossing Tower Bridge and cruising past the Tower of London, entering the lion's den, the financial quarter known as the City, in a series of underpasses on the north bank. Again, I think, to ignore the influence of the fellows in bowler hats would be to ignore the place of England in the world. The City, like the country, is small, but fighting well above its weight, perhaps arrogantly, making a small minority beyond wealthy with the benefit of louche and creative accounting, lax tax laws and favourable governance. Meanwhile, sadly, the rest of us – all in it together,

of course – suffocate under an austerity caused by doomed deals that, ultimately, lead to the closure of hospitals, schools and public toilets. Try to find a public convenience that's open in the provinces these days and you'll begin to understand the place of the City in modern England (trust me, I have tried). Still, I think, lighten up: the City exists and is to be admired, if not for its morals then certainly for its architecture.

London is here in its newness, all glinting glass, shards of vertical light and modernist architecture contrasting with the austere stone and brick that showed off medieval wealth. No matter what political machinations are taking place in Westminster, it's still a thrill to be here, driving down the Embankment with the Thames to my left, soaking up this marvellous, terrible, enormous, exciting city as it sparkles in the morning sun.

On the opposite side of the river I see the South Bank, both a skateboarding hangout and a place of culture and art: the Royal Festival Hall, the Hayward Gallery, the National Theatre. When my children were young they loved coming here, to enjoy ice creams, to visit the fish at the Sea Life Aquarium and to see the city from the best seat in the house: the London Eye. It was the best of the city and I am glad to have been able to show them so that they aren't afraid of it, should they ever

want to come here to work or study. People don't talk on the Tube, it's true, but it doesn't make it all bad.

I snap a shot of the giant Ferris wheel through the swishing leaves of the plane trees that line the Embankment. They're a pain for the wandering campervanner looking to take the perfect photo, but they create a gorgeous avenue of pollution-swallowing green and dappled light all along this side of the river.

I arrive at the lights where the Embankment meets Westminster Bridge. Big Ben is right in front of me, the whole tower sadly covered in scaffolding, so the picture isn't worth taking. I drive around Parliament Square and back on to the Embankment past Tate Britain, Battersea Park and Vauxhall Bridge before crossing over Battersea Bridge towards Wandsworth, Putney and Richmond.

I continue onwards, finding the roads that pass the closest to the river: through Teddington, Hampton, Sunbury, Egham and Old Windsor. At Runnymede, the place where the Magna Carta was signed, I stop in a big grassy car park that borders the river. It's hot, so I think about swimming. But the current is strong by the looks of it, so I carry on, through Bray and Maidenhead to Cookham, Marlow, Henley (the Royal Regatta is on and it

smells of Prosecco when I get out of the van to snap pics), Caversham and Goring.

At Henley I find the dream of England that brings so many here. Floppy-hatted women teeter along the riverside with stemmed glasses in their hands while boatered and stripey-jacketed hoons (for want of a more English word, but good because it's a classless insult) bray at them from expensive cruisers: Well hello, ladies! Behind them, unnoticed, go the coxless pairs in a pageant that, at first glance, looks more about socialising than about rowing.

I get the shot and move along.

The further I get from the city the more the landscape changes, with open fields and parkland bordering the river. There are private estates and perfect villages, bunting-decked high streets and riverside cafés. At Cookham there is a pub overlooking the water; it's the same at Boulter's Lock in Maidenhead. At Goring, a little café right next to the bridge seats women in flowery summer dresses and men in pink shirts and panamas.

I reach Abingdon and cross the bridge on to the southern bank, where I find the perfect park-up spot adjacent to the river, at the cricket club. A game is in full swing so I stop to look. All the clichés are here as the willow clips the leather on its way to the boundary. Howzat?! I think of where I have been and what this game and these cricketers, happily living an

idyll in the summer sunshine, mean to the rest of us. Can you have the cricket without also having the city? Is it possible to enjoy the countryside without the urbanisation? Would the slow road be anything without the motorway?

I think I know the answer as I strip off and slip into the green water just downstream from Abingdon Lock for my first-ever swim in the Thames. It's heavenly, quite simply lovely, and I am grateful for the hot day and the traffic that have made it so. A true slow-road adventure with a perfect finish.

# THE DRIVING

I thought the same thing as you when I decided to take on the Thames. But then, the more I drove the more I realised that it is an essential journey through the heart of the city and out into the heart of England. I grew up near the Thames, in cosy Middle England, so I know the places well. I also lived in London, so I know it well too. But if you don't know the area and aren't afraid of traffic, then I urge you to do it. The driving is slow and painful in places but glorious in others. You will encounter traffic and lights and confusing roundabouts, but don't let them put you off. London flows more freely now than two years ago and it isn't that bad. Just keep your nerve, don't let the city drivers bully you, and enjoy it for what it is – a leisurely journey up England's oldest and finest thoroughfare.

If you have never visited London, then this is your excuse to fly past the monuments and special places that you just can't ignore. Westminster, whatever it stands for, is important, as are Greenwich, the Tower, Big Ben, Hampton Court Palace and even Windsor. It would take a you a few weeks to do the lot if you wanted to follow the tourist trail, but this way you can dip in and out of the attractions as you like because you're passing them anyway.

Even if you don't follow my route to the letter – I skipped a few of the bends to make it a little more direct – the principle is the same: follow the river as close as you can. Don't miss the Embankment from the Tower of London to Battersea Bridge, the section between Teddington and Hampton Court – or the little section after Hampton which takes you past Sunbury Lock. Also on the hit list are Runnymede, Old Windsor, Eton, Oakley Green and Bray, as well as Cookham, Boulter's Lock and Henley. The section between Marlow and Henley is a world away from the city, which is what makes this such an invigorating run. Just don't forget, when you are enjoying the leafy 'burbs of Berkshire and Oxfordshire, to pay the congestion charge before midnight on the day after you passed through the Congestion Charge Zone that covers the heart of London (unless you travelled through at the weekend or in the evening, when it is free).

The first part of the drive isn't the prettiest. Leaving the A282 (the Dartford Crossing stretch of the M25) at junction 1A, follow the A206 as far as Greenwich Market (just after the meridian), and then take the A200, which will take you through Surrey Quays and on to Bermondsey, where you'll go into a one-way system, with a right turn to Tower Bridge Road. Going over Tower Bridge is a thrill in itself, which only gets better as you pass the Tower of London on your left, straight away, before turning left on to Lower Thames Street (the A3211). This turns into the Embankment and whizzes you all the way to Parliament Square, where you pick up the A3212, Millbank, which soon changes to Gloucester Road. Cross the river at Battersea Bridge, which isn't the prettiest but can take your weight. Once on the south side, follow Battersea Bridge Road on to the A3205, then the A217 and the A3 for a short while before taking a right to Putney Bridge Road, which will take you to Lower Richmond Road and then Mortlake High Street and lead you to the A316. This will take you through Richmond, over the old Richmond Bridge and on to the A305 Richmond Road, then

the A310 Twickenham Road, which will take you past Hampton Court Palace. After the palace, take a right at the mini-roundabout on the Hampton Court Road, then keep your eyes peeled for a left turn to East Sunbury (Lower Sunbury). This will take you along a pretty stretch between treatment works, reservoirs and Sunbury Lock and will lead you nicely to Shepperton and Chertsey before offering you the chance to take the A308 Staines Road (heading west rather than south to Kingston upon Thames). Follow this through Windsor and then head out towards Eton and Dorney, crossing the river again on the B3021 to Datchet (where it becomes the B470), and then again at the Home Park to take you right past Windsor Castle. Thereafter it's a bit of a widdle to get back on to the A308, which will take you under the M4 and on to Maidenhead. In Maidenhead you'll need to follow the one-way system to the Bath Road and Taplow, turning off left upstream at the A4094 to Cookham. At Bourne End this changes to the A4155 and takes you through some delightful scenery and countryside to Marlow and Henley. Reading, which is your next conurbation after Henley, is a bit tricky and busy, but follow the signs for the A329 Oxford Road/Pangbourne and you'll head out of town along the river as far as Goring, where you can take a nice riverside detour by taking the B4009 over the river and north towards Crowmarsh Gifford, where you pick up the busier A4074. Turn left on the A415 and head into Abingdon. The cricket club, your final destination, in on the left just before the bridge. Rest and relax.

That was fun, wasn't it? Hope you remembered a map, and perhaps your satnav.

## PLACES TO STAY

**Abbey Wood Caravan Club Site**
Federation Road, London, SE2 OLS
**tel:** 020 8311 7708

**info:** *A Caravan and Motorhome Club Site just off the A206. Perfectly situated at the start (or end) of this route. Also handy if you want to day trip into London without worrying about parking. Book early as it is popular.*

**Henley Four Oaks
Caravan Club Site**
Marlow Road, Henley-on-Thames,
Oxfordshire, RG9 2HY
**tel:** 01491 572312

**info:** *Right on the A4155, so perfect for overnights to explore Henley, Marlow and the Chilterns.*

**Northmoor Lock Paddocks**
Barefoot Campsites, Badswell Lane,
Appleton, Oxfordshire, OX13 5JN
**email:** campingonthethames@gmail.com
**tel:** 07961 514047

**info:** *Short-wheel-based campers only at this riverside idyll upstream from Abingdon.*

**Hurley Riverside Park**
Hurley, Berkshire, SL6 5NE
**web:** www.hurleyriversidepark.co.uk
**email:** info@hurleyriversidepark.co.uk
**tel:** 01628 824493

**info:** *A formal campsite between Bisham and Henley with all the trimmings, but – and it's a great big, fantastic but – it's on the river!*

# IN THE AREA

Take your pick! There is just about everything 'in the area' on this route, simply because it's London, and London is one of the world's biggest and most visited cities. So you can choose any kind of restaurant, any kind of pub or café, any type of art or culture you fancy. You can visit palaces, cathedrals and castles, shop until you droop, laze by the river, swim, run cycle. And you can do it all on this route! Highlights include:

**National Maritime Museum and Greenwich Royal Observatory** for all things nautical and astronomical in the beautiful Greenwich Park • www.rmg.co.uk

**Tate Modern** for modern art in the old Bankside Power Station. • www.tate.org.uk/visit/tate-modern

**Tate Britain** for British Art from 1500 to the present day. • www.tate.org.uk/visit/tate-britain

**Tower of London** for the Crown Jewels, dungeons and lots of local events. • www.hrp.org.uk

**Hampton Court Palace** for gardens and grandeur. • www.hrp.org.uk

**The London Eye** the best way to see the skyline from the South Bank. • www.londoneye.com

**The Royal Festival Hall and South Bank Centre** for all things cultural – music, art and life. • www.southbankcentre.co.uk

**Sea Life London Aquarium** – massive aquarium with sharks, right opposite Parliament. • www.visitsealife.com/london

**The Thames Path** for those who might like to park up and get out and walk once in a while. • www.thames-path.org.uk

**Royal Botanic Gardens Kew** – the world's biggest Victorian greenhouse is just the start of this botanical wonderland. • www.kew.org

**Windsor Castle** One of Her Madge's royal hangouts and home to royals of all flavours for over 1,000 years. Popular with tourists, always busy and always worth a peep. • www.windsor.gov.uk

Nearest van hire

**CamperVanTastic Ltd**
• www.campervantastic.com

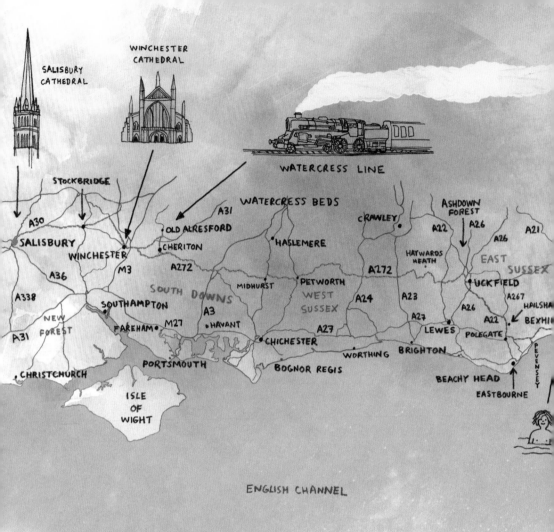

SALISBURY
CATHEDRAL

WINCHESTER
CATHEDRAL

WATERCRESS LINE

STOCKBRIDGE

WATERCRESS BEDS

A31
OLD ALRESFORD

CRAWLEY

ASHDOWN
FOREST

A22    A26

A26    A21

A30

SALISBURY

CHERITON

HASLEMERE

HAYWARDS
HEATH

EAST

SUSSEX

WINCHESTER

A272

M3

A272

UCKFIELD

A36

MIDHURST

PETWORTH

A24

A23

A267

A338

SOUTH DOWNS

WEST

SUSSEX

A26

HAILSHAM

SOUTHAMPTON

A3

A27

BEXHILL

NEW

FAREHAM

M27

HAVANT

A27

LEWES

A22

POLEGATE

A31

FOREST

CHICHESTER

BOGNOR REGIS

WORTHING

BRIGHTON

CHRISTCHURCH

PORTSMOUTH

BEACHY HEAD

EASTBOURNE

PEVENSEY

ISLE
OF
WIGHT

ENGLISH CHANNEL

# ROUTE 10

the church spire and town-hall clock frame the back ground. Click: this is England. In the clear water a few huge trout swim against the flow. On a raft of weed I see a water vole preening itself. I am surprised to see such enormous fish and elusive mammals right in the middle of a town, but then again, I think, it wouldn't be such an idyll without them. They make the picture perfect.

I leave Stockbridge and head on, further along the A30, turning on to the A272 in the direction of Winchester, where a little wiggling gets me to the A272 the other side of the A34, heading towards Petersfield. On the way I notice a sign for Alresford and take a left towards it, almost automatically. This is because I am feeling the pull of my long-dead elders, finding, it seems, my own pilgrim route. Old Alresford is the home of the Doreys, my ancestral home, the seat of all things Dorey. It is the place where my father, my grandfather and my grandmother (and the rest of them) are buried. I owe it to them to pay a visit, so I follow my nose, even though I haven't been here in many years, and find my way to town.

New Alresford is unchanged. It is another of those lovely, well-to-do, Middle England villages. Its high street appears healthy, with butchers, bakers, florists and gift shops lining a wide, straight, low-rise centre.

I take a left towards Old Alresford and drive down a broad, shady, tree-lined street with hanging baskets dripping colour from every lamp post.

I arrive at St Mary the Virgin Church and park. Walking through the lychgate, I gasp at the beauty of the place. It's astounding. On one side is the road, on another a rusting wrought-iron fence, and on a third an old red-brick wall, separating the churchyard from the manor house. Between the road, rails and wall lie the 19th-century church and the graveyard. There

are trees standing tall among the well-weathered and worn gravestones: copper beech and yew catch my eye. The church is built of brick and decorative flint, with a square turreted tower. The grass has been neatly cut and the only things that seem a little out of order are the odd wonky headstones, tilted with the settling of the earth. My lot are somewhere in the far corner, beneath an elm, so I go over to find them. After a while I see the headstone that belongs to them all. It's been a while since anyone was here, so I clear away the weeds, fill up the urn with water and head off looking for something to put in it.

My forebears were farmers here in Alresford. They farmed watercress in the shallow beds fed by the River Alre and sent it to London on the now-famous Watercress Line. The railway opened in 1865 and was officially known as the Mid-Hants Railway. It served Alresford, joining it to the main line at Alton. During its heyday, the line enabled the watercress farmers of Alresford to get their crop to the markets in London every day.

I walk down a small lane that I know connects the church to Arle Mill and the watercress beds. They look overgrown and neglected these days, a sad reflection of the way we farm and eat, I guess. An honesty box next to a rusty old fridge offers watercress for 50p a bunch.

I pick some cress from the beds (for once I feel entitled), a few heads of meadowsweet, some bittersweet and some greater willowherb and make a wild posy. I walk back to the grave and place it in the urn. I have a chat with my grandmother, who I spent many happy summers with at Petersfield when I was a boy. We talk about a few things and then I leave them all be. When I return to the van I find I have tears staining my cheeks because I know I will never end up here in this lovely corner of England. I wish for things to be different and, besides, I am the last male in my line. I am not alone in my life, but it still hurts to be the last and only one remaining.

I get back in the van and turn on the iPod. 'Fisherman's Blues' is still on repeat. I hit open country and wind down the window. The fields of flax and corn fly by as I make my way along this heavenly historic route, following the original Pilgrims' Way towards the South Downs.

I feel a little sad when I get to Uckfield and the end of the A272, so I turn the van to the south, towards Bexhill. I make my way, slowly, to the sea, to finish my pilgrimage with a cleansing dip. I remove my clothes, leave them in a neat pile on one of the wave-worn groynes and hobble over the shingle into a murky English Channel with a sharp intake of breath.

# THE DRIVING

NOTE: The A272 has varying speed limits, which can be a hazard. Although we are on the slow road and always mindful of the dawdling necessary to enjoy it properly, it is easy to get caught out transitioning from the national speed limit to a 30mph zone. I did. Just saying.

When I first found out about this route I was looking for something that reeked of England. It needed to be somewhere in the south and it needed to be authentic, without too much fussing about with roundabouts and traffic lights. I wanted to drive through lovely countryside, to see a few villages and to feel that I was part of a landscape with ancient connections that wasn't ravaged by development or bypasses. As it is, you can't quite escape the trunk roads, especially if you choose to skirt Winchester and Salisbury. At times, due to the way the roads have been developed, you have to spend a few miserable miles between cuttings on the A31 or the A36, but it's worth the misery: the rest of this route is a joy.

I started on the A303 as I was coming from my home in Cornwall, taking the A360 just before Stonehenge towards Salisbury before picking up the A30 towards Stockbridge. The sections before Salisbury are long and straight, with lovely views miles and miles in front. It's open country consisting of farmland, copse and rolling hills. The skies are big.

After Stockbridge the A30 continues to amble along through farmland until the rather unassuming junction with the A272, which heads off uphill along a corridor of tall, overgrown hedgerows until it arrives at the junction with the A34. This isn't the best bit, but needs must: follow the A34 and head for the A31, along a short stretch of the A272. Then it's on to the A31. You don't have to stay on it for long, as it soon offers you absolution from the heavy traffic in the form of the serenity of the A272 again.

Now you're in the South Downs National Park the landscape changes. The hills are still on the gentle side, but the road has more curves and weaves its way through hamlets and villages along the way. At Petersfield it loses its way a little, but it's nothing to pass through the town and head out on the B2070 London Road before taking a right on to the A272 again.

Through more villages, then it's on to Trotten Common, an area of birch, fir and scrub gorse, before arriving at Midhurst. Again, the A272 here is truncated by newer roads so you'll have to navigate your way up the A286 to find it again. This is the way with the A272. It's a cross-country route, which means that it bisects the major routes going north to south that radiate away from London. All along its length they take priority, meaning that the A272 seems like an afterthought.

But it really isn't an afterthought! The A272 takes you past lovely parkland at Petworth and through incredibly picturesque villages like Wisborough Green, a divine spot with red-brick-and-clay-tile houses

surrounding a village green and cricket pitch with a superb pub close by. Floral displays abound, while the Union Jack flutters in the breeze next to the war memorial. It screams 'England!' at you, with the roses around the door turned up to eleven and Miss Marple – and probably Inspector Morse as well – ready to pounce should you ever find yourself transformed into a Midsomer murderer. Pop a penny in the honesty box for fresh veg, marigolds and marmalade.

Don't worry if you miss the Three Crowns at Wisborough Green. There are plenty of other boozers along this route, complete with swinging sign, National Trust–coloured paintwork and picnic tables outside. There aren't many petrol stations or supermarkets, except in the bigger towns, which is another element that makes this lovely little half-forgotten road in southern England such a draw. It's relatively unspoilt, a fine example of England's towns and villages at their most genteel.

It's a bit of a disappointment to get to Haywards Heath and find the A272 becomes a ring road with goodness knows how many mini-roundabouts, but still it marches on, stoically crossing the A275 and A22, defiant in the face of oncoming modernity, until it stops ignominiously when it reaches the junction with the A267 north of Eastbourne.

But of course this is where you can take a right and head to the coast on the A267, which meets the A22 and then the A27 (which becomes the A259) to Bexhill. It is busy and oversubscribed on this route, but it's worth it for the sight of the sea, the English coastal architecture and a peep at England's south coast. If you're going looking for England, you might as well go the whole way.

## PLACES TO STAY

**Morn Hill Caravan Club Site**
Alresford Road, Winchester, Hampshire,
SO21 1HL
**tel:** 01962 869877

**info:** *Caravan and Motorhome Club Site just a short drive from Winchester.*

**The Crown Inn**
Cholderton, Wiltshire, SP4 0DW
**web:** www.crowncholderton.com
**email:** info@crowncholderton.com
**tel:** 01980 629247

**info:** *A friendly Britstop with a huge car park and a grassy area to overlook. No loos, but great beer.*

**Horam Manor Touring Park**
Horam, Heathfield, East Sussex, TN21 0YD
**web:** www.horam-manor.co.uk
**email:** camping@horam-manor.co.uk
**tel:** 01435 813662

**info:** *Large family-run park on a manor estate with fishing, café, riding and tennis.*

**The White Hart**
Darwell Lane, Netherfield, Nr Battle,
East Sussex, TN33 9QH
**web:** www.thewhitehartnetherfield.com
**email:** hello@thewhitehartnetherfield.com
**tel:** 01424 838382

**info:** *A Britstop on the South Downs with a great car park overlooking the south coast. Great food. Nice people. Top views from the fantastic terrace.*

# IN THE AREA

**Watercress Line**  This is the branch line that enabled watercress farmers like the Doreys to send their produce to London. Now run by volunteers and running regular steam trains (and Thomas the Tank Engine!). Plus vintage fairground rides.  • www.watercressline.co.uk

**Bluebell Railway**  Another fab heritage railway near East Grinstead, offering train rides and more from its volunteer-run lines and platforms. Great stuff!  • www.bluebell-railway.com

**Petworth Park**  Seven hundred acres of parkland and gardens, the National Trust's finest art collection, an incredible stately home and even a connection to the Gunpowder Plot. Crikey.  • www.nationaltrust.org.uk/petworth-house-and-park

**Winchester Cathedral**  The final resting place of King Alfred the Great, King Cnut and even Jane Austen. Winchester was once the religious hub of Wessex, a diocese stretching from the Thames to the English Channel.  • www.winchester-cathedral.org.uk

## Salisbury Cathedral

With Britain's tallest spire, Salisbury Cathedral has long been a landmark in Old Sarum. As a child, I used to call it strawberry needle when we visited. The best preserved of the only four existing copies of the Magna Carta resides at Salisbury. This is still a place of pilgrimage, if only to admire the medieval architecture.

• www.salisburycathedral.org.uk

## De La Warr Pavilion,
**Bexhill** An incredible 1930s building that's home to a thriving arts centre and performance space. Go for the views, or the art, or the music, or just to take five minutes to look at the sea. Glorious. A cathedral of secular loveliness.

• www.dlwp.com

**Stonehenge** Another cathedral, of sorts, but dating back quite a lot further than Winchester or Salisbury. Stonehenge is one of the world's most famous Neolithic sites and continues to inspire wonderment and awe, even if you can't hug the stones any more. • www.english-heritage.org.uk/visit/places/stonehenge

**Woodhenge** The wood may have been replaced by concrete markers, but at least you can walk among them. Another fantastic ancient site.

• www.english-heritage.org.uk/visit/places/woodhenge

Nearest van hire

**Moovans Campervan Rentals**
• www.moovans.com

147

**EAST ANGLIA**

East Anglia is flat. But that
doesn't mean it hasn't got drama. Norfolk
has plenty, from windmills to seal colonies, beach
huts on stilts and classic seaside towns. There is great
camping, great food and a few great pubs. What more could
you want from a road trip? Head south and things change.
Find Britain at its holiday best in Great Yarmouth by riding
one of the UK's oldest wooden rollercoasters, or by seeing
how they make seaside rock. Then, when you get to
Southwold, see how it can be subverted in the
Under the Pier Show. There are beach huts
there, too, of course.

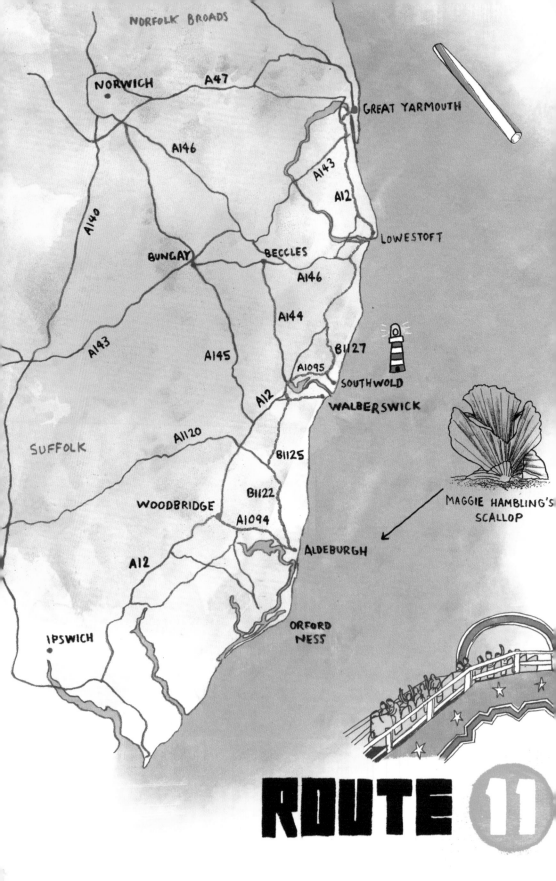

NORFOLK BROADS

NORWICH

A47

GREAT YARMOUTH

A146

A143

A12

LOWESTOFT

A140

BUNGAY

BECCLES

A146

A144

A143

A145

A12

A1095

B1127

SOUTHWOLD

WALBERSWICK

SUFFOLK

A1120

B1125

MAGGIE HAMBLING'S SCALLOP

WOODBRIDGE

B1122

A1094

A12

ALDEBURGH

IPSWICH

ORFORD NESS

ROUTE 11

# THE DRIVING

I'm not going to lie to you. The spine of the Suffolk coast is, unfortunately, the hideous ribbon of tarmacked hatred that is the A12. It's been voted Britain's worst road in a few damning polls, thanks to constant roadworks and potholes.

So why, then, are we looking to travel up it for this route? Well, because there's no other way of linking Aldeburgh, Southwold and Great Yarmouth. You can avoid besmirching your motorhome's tyres on the despised asphalt of the A12 in places, but you just can't do without it. Which is a shame really, because between the A12 and the sea lies a beautiful, varied and fascinating stretch of coastline. There's no coast road, just a series of small villages and stop-offs along the way that you simply must go and see.

The coast here offers enormous contrast, from the tranquillity of Minsmere (where the BBC programme *Springwatch* is filmed) to the quaint and yet classy Southwold, from the broken-down church of St Andrew at Covehithe to the brashness of lost glory that exists at Great Yarmouth.

Between the 1930s roller coaster and some of the country's most expensive beach huts is a coast that's eroding fast, has a great deal of diversity and is a great place to escape the rat lanes of the A12.

Heading north on the A12, come off it as soon as you can after the roundabouted quagmire that the Woodbridge bypass gives you and head east on the A1152 towards Rendlesham, and from there to Tunstall and then Church Common on the A1152 and the B1069. This will bring you out on the Aldeburgh Road (the A1094, which will take you straight to Aldeburgh). My first port of call would always be to check out Maggi Hambling's scallop shell sculpture memorial to Benjamin Britten. It's been vandalised many times since it was installed in 2003. Some claim it ruins a gloriously unspoiled part of the coast, but I really love it and would hate to see it destroyed or moved.

From Aldeburgh there's a lovely section of coastal road to Thorpeness. Then you'll have to follow the B1353 and then the B1122 which becomes the B1125 and then heads off across country towards Walberswick. This tiny village was once the poor cousin to neighbouring Southwold, but it's firmly on the map these days. It sits on the south side of the River Blyth and has pubs, chippies and the ubiquitous galleries. A ferry takes you across the river to Southwold's delightful working harbour. But before you go all the way there, check out the RSPB reserve at Minsmere for the UK's rarest wildlife and seek out the lost city of Dunwich, once the capital of East Anglia.

Once at Walberswick you'll have to retrace your steps if you want to get your wagon across the River Blyth. So head back to the A12 and then take the A1095 into Southwold. From there, for camping, head south along the beach towards Reydon Marshes. This will bring you to the river again and a collection of very picturesque fishing huts, a great pub and the ferry back to Walberswick.

You can head to the wonderfully named Wangford if you want to continue north, although you can put off taking the A12 by heading north on the B1127 to South Cove and Covehithe, where the lovely ruined church will give you the willies. You can carry on along the road (on foot please), but beware, as it stops rather abruptly at the cliff – the rest of the road is in the sea somewhere.

Sadly you're on the A12 again after Covehithe, although there are diversions en route that will take you along the coast: after the harbour at Lowestoft you can take the Corton Road along Corton Cliffs (back to the A12) and then head back on Marine Parade at Gorleston-on-Sea. It's a different kind of coast here from Southwold: built up, with elegant Victorian mansions standing side by side with mock Tudor 1930s homes and modern townhouses overlooking the sea, green spaces, tennis courts and palm trees. A far cry from the tiny fishermen's cottages of the Suffolk coast further south.

It's another story still over the water at Great Yarmouth. Cross the river on the A1243 and follow it to the south towards South Denes, through

the working harbour and warehouses, on to South Beach Parade. It's fully industrialised and weary here, around the harbour, with barbed-wire fences, car lots and warehouses. The first sign of any kind of glamour here is the Pleasure Beach. It sits uncomfortably between the terraced houses and the sea, behind a brick wall topped with razor wire. Don't be put off, though. Behind that brick wall stands a sturdy relic of fun times gone by. The bright blue–painted sides of The Scenic – protruding above the wire – show you that you've made it to the place where dreams can come true. Leave your inhibitions at the van, cast aside your jaded view of the world and take a ride on something truly special.

Scream if you want to go faster.

## PLACES TO STAY

**Southwold Camp Site**
Ferry Road, Southwold, Suffolk, IP18 6ND
**web:** www.southwoldcamping.com
**tel:** 01502 722486

**info:** *Council owned and very popular. Make a booking and then take your place at this lovely campsite south of Southwold.*

**Brick Kiln Farm Campsite**
Brick Kiln Cottage, Campsea Ashe,
Woodbridge, Suffolk, IP13 0QL
**web:** www.brickkilnfarmsuffolk.co.uk
**email:** info@brickkilnfarmsuffolk.co.uk
**tel:** 01728 747281

**info:** *Near Woodbridge, handy for the A12 (eww) but lovely all the same. Quirky and interesting, just the way we like it.*

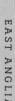

Nearest van hire

**Suffolk Camper Van Hire**
• www.suffolkcampervanhire.co.uk

# IN THE AREA

**Southwold Pier**  A fabulous pier, with all the right bits, some tackiness, some fish and chips and the always amazing Under the Pier Show.
• www.underthepier.com  and  • www.southwoldpier.co.uk

**Pleasure Beach, Great Yarmouth**  Yes, it can smell of chips and yes, there will be some stuff you'll find tacky and awful, but this is the real deal. Ride The Scenic, let your inhibitions go!  • www.pleasure-beach.co.uk

**Minsmere RSPB Reserve**  Great chance of seeing Britain's rarest from the hides and the possibility of seeing an otter in the reed beds ... brilliant and very peaceful.  • www.rspb.org.uk/reserves-and-events/reserves-a-z/minsmere

**Sea Life, Great Yarmouth**  Crocs, penguins and sharks, but not in the same enclosure, thankfully, at this classic aquarium.  • www.visitsealife.com/great-yarmouth

**Orford Castle**  One of the UK's most complete castles without a royal living in it. Well, not a living one anyway, although legend has it that it's a merman, not a king, who haunts the castle...
• www.english-heritage.org.uk/visit/places/orford-castle

**Docwras Rock Factory, Great Yarmouth**  See lettered rock being made and find out its secrets. Why does the rock maker have missing fingers? Do they ever make spelling mistakes?
• www.facebook.com/pages/Docwras-Rock-Factory/160303970652861

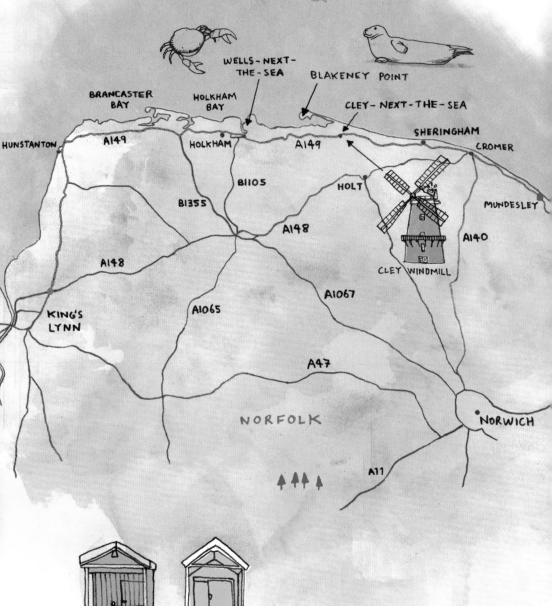

NORTH SEA

BRANCASTER BAY

HOLKHAM BAY

WELLS-NEXT-THE-SEA

BLAKENEY POINT

CLEY-NEXT-THE-SEA

SHERINGHAM

HUNSTANTON

A149

HOLKHAM

A149

CROMER

B1105

HOLT

MUNDESLEY

B1355

A148

CLEY WINDMILL

A140

A148

A1067

KING'S LYNN

A1065

A47

NORFOLK

NORWICH

A11

ROUTE **12**

# NORTH NORFOLK

## DRIVING DOWN MEMORY LANE

The north coast of Norfolk is magnificent. It's largely flat but never dull. The coast road between King's Lynn meanders and wiggles its way along the north coast to Great Yarmouth, changing all the time as it goes. From the salt marshes at Cley to the cliffs at Cromer, it's a meanderer's delight.

**BEST FOR:**
Wending your way along the coast

START: King's Lynn

END: Mundesley

MILEAGE: 60 miles (96 kilometres)

DAYS TO EXPLORE: 3

OS LANDRANGER MAP: 132, 133

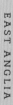

EAST ANGLIA

I slept in the van in a small lay-by at the side of a minor road just off the A149 and have woken early. I want to make the most of the day. It's bright, breezy and cool, with brilliant spring sunshine backlighting the vivid greens of new leaves on the beeches in the hedgerows.

It's been a while since I have been here. The last time I drove this stretch of coast I was here to film my TV series, *One Man and His Campervan*, in 2010. So little has changed since then that it could have been yesterday. By the time I get to Brancaster I'm feeling a little nostalgic for the old Type 2 camper van that I drove in the series. Norfolk was perfect country for it. As it chugged along, powered by its whistling flat-4 engine, it felt like nothing

could stop us. While not much of a climber, the old air-cooled engine loved the winding flats, pushing around corners with the flowing confidence of an old girl who had never lost the twinkle in her eye and was let out to play again.

At Wells-next-the-Sea I park up looking for somewhere to grab a cup of tea and stumble upon the workshops of Whin Hill Cider, the makers of a very fine Norfolk brew that I drank in large quantities one night after filming an episode of the show. I had been left by the film crew in an orchard by a pond, with a fire and a crate of Whin Hill's finest batch. With nothing much else to do except stoke the fire and quaff the merchandise, I enjoyed a solo night out under the brightest of starry nights. It was warm and dry, I was earning money, I had cider and I was driving a 1979 camper van that had made its way up from Devon via the New Forest with barely a murmur. This was good.

At Brancaster I find myself on the road to the Royal Norfolk Golf Club. It's a dry day and yet the roadway is wet. It's low lying. When I get to the car park I see that there is a caravan on bricks in the car park. I wonder why. I spend some time on the beach and then make to leave, but as I do so I notice the water is creeping around the van's wheels. The puddles on the road are bigger, and in some places the road is covered. The tide is coming in. What do I do? Rather than sitting it out, I opt to push on, ploughing through the approaching waters, making a bow wave as the tide threatens to engulf the road. I feel like Moses in reverse. The wave grows and I am thankful that I don't stall. Walkers, stomping by from the safety of a high dyke, wave as I splash by.

At the quayside in Brancaster I get out of the van to see how high the tide has reached. It is lapping against the road, engulfing footpaths and filling the muddy creeks.

I take pictures of a crab shack and recall the crab fisherman I met during the filming of the TV show who had never eaten crab – despite catching it for all of his working life – and the complaints I had from viewers when I boiled one for my tea. I also remember the tea itself, cooked at the campsite at Stiffkey overlooking the marshes. I served up the crab meat with delicious freshly picked samphire and a risotto made with stock from

wild fennel. I ate it, cold, after the film crew had got all the shots they wanted and left me to my own devices for the night. Those were the nights I loved, and they were the very best moments about making a TV show: time to be alone, to come down after the high anxiety of performing and cooking for the camera. A time to ring my daughters and talk to them about how their days had been.

I walk to the beach at Wells to find the famous beach huts on stilts where my friends and I spent time walking and playing. For a few years I went to Norfolk regularly to visit my best friend, who was attending college in King's Lynn and was holed up in a tiny cottage in Binham, not far from there. We'd lose days drinking, smoking and writing music for our 'album', a single cassette of songs about girls and heartache that never made it to the charts. On the way back from the pub we'd try cow tipping, scaring ourselves in the ruined priory and falling over into deep muddy ditches. On headache-ruined days we'd wander down to the beach at Wells to squint at the colourful beach huts on stilts.

The beach is sunny and lovely today, the beach huts just as bright and cheery as they were back then. I can see why images of them grace tourist brochures and why the wealthy seek them out, even with price tags of up to £70,000. It must be a lovely spot to while away the days.

Sadly I can't, so I press on, towards West Runton, Cromer and then Overstrand, where I park up in the car park overlooking the beach and wander down to the café to pick up something for lunch. It's buzzing, even though the beach is quiet. It seems the whole of Norfolk's coastal walkers are here for the day. I grab a table by the window and sit with my cuppa. Looking out, I can see the sea beyond the breakers at the foot of the cliff. The tide has gone out again and I wonder if I'll have time to get back to Brancaster to take the photograph I need before I get cut off again.

# THE DRIVING

The A149 leaves King's Lynn as a major A road, wide and strong as it bypasses Sandringham and enters Dersingham Bog, with woods either side of the road. It bypasses Dersingham, Ingoldisthorpe and Snettisham before trundling on to Hunstanton on a long, straight stretch that passes lavender fields and rapeseed. A diversion into Hunstanton reveals a Victorian resort with shabby edges, but still looking splendid in the sun. After Hunstanton the road turns east and starts to slow down a little: there are no bypasses from here, so you'll pootle through tiny villages on the edge of the marshes which stretch off to the north in seemingly impenetrable networks of creeks, mud flats and steep muddy banks.

A couple of dog-legs at Burnham lead you to the most celebrated part of the Norfolk coast. First comes Holkham, then Wells-next-the-Sea, Stiffkey, Blakeney and Cley. Here it can be narrow, but it's no harder to drive: just take it easy. In summer you'll pass verges full of poppies, fennel and daisies, as well as escapees from fields of rape. On this stretch, the geography makes it easier for beach walks. The marshes give way to

shingle and sandbanks, with access by vehicle at Cley, your first opportunity since Hunstanton to park up with a sea view. Then it's a pootle towards Sheringham and slightly higher ground, and at least a bit of a cliff to fall down. Here, to counter longshore drift there are groynes and sea defences and it starts to feel very seasidey all of a sudden. It's busy and buzzing, and the one-way system will take you into lots of impossible corners if you let it. Best park and walk if you need to pick up souvenirs or supplies. And then on, to the Runtons, home of 'legendary' surf breaks and more groynes, before you hit the peak of the seaside at Cromer, a Victorian resort, recumbent and resplendent with pier, arcades and fish and chippers galore. There is a great place to park up before the town at the Runton Road NNDC Car Park. Great views but sadly no overnighting. I'd happily pay a tenner to sleep in the van there if it was allowed, in the process giving the council much-needed cash when the car park would otherwise be empty, but no, we're stuck in the dark ages here too. Campsites only. Come on, councils of England! When will you wake up to this? We want to stay – and spend our money – but we don't want to be forced into campsites. Grrrr. We're not all yobs and ne'er-do-wells.

At Cromer the A149 makes a dash for Norwich, but our route presses on eastwards on the Overstrand Road. You'll need to keep your eyes open for the turn-off to the left, at a mini-roundabout, signposted to Mundesley and Overstrand. Then you're off to explore a series of lovely little beach towns, each perched atop a cliff. It's widdly and winding until you get to Mundesley, which is where I turned and headed for Norwich. It's a forgotten corner of England, and for that reason it's worth a look. Just don't get stuck in Norwich. And you will!

### Nearest van hire

**Retro Campers Norfolk**
- www.retrocampersnorfolk.co.uk

# IN THE AREA

**Wells and Walsingham Light Railway**  The smallest ten-and-a-half-inch-gauge railway in the world. Runs steam and diesel between Wells and Walsingham. And a great café too!  • **www.wwlr.co.uk**

**North Norfolk Railway**  Five miles of full-sized steam power on the Poppy Line between Sheringham and Holt.  • **www.nnrailway.co.uk**

**Blakeney Seal Trips** At Blakeney Point there is a colony of seals. It is possible to go and see them by boat from Blakeney or Morston on an approved seal-watching tour. Beans Boats are well established, but there are lots of other operators as well.

- www.beansboattrips.co.uk
- www.bishopsboats.com

**Wiveton Hall** Posh, unashamed and a bit mad. Plus a great farm shop and restaurant, along with owner-led tours of the grand old house that dates back to 1652.

- www.wivetonhall.co.uk

## PLACES TO STAY

**Blue Skies Campsite**
Stiffkey Road, Wells-next-the-Sea, Norfolk, NR23 1QB
**web:** www.blueskiescampsite.co.uk
**email:** info@blueskiescampsite.co.uk
**tel:** 07557 021660

**info:** *A campsite that will make you smile as you drive past and decide to pull a U-turn. Sunny, friendly and fun (and bigger than it looks).*

**High Sand Creek**
Greenway, Stiffkey, Norfolk, NR23 1QF
**web:** www.highsandcreekcampsite stiffkey.co.uk
**tel:** 01328 830235

**info:** *Another darling of the 'cool camping' scene. Rightly so, as it's on the creek and just a dash from the marshes. Great sunsets too, as it's on a gently sloping field.*

**Seacroft Caravan Club Site**
Cromer Road, East Runton, Norfolk, NR27 9NH
**tel:** 01263 514938

**info:** *It has a bar. And a pool. Need more?*

# THE MIDLANDS

Slap bang in the middle of the
Midlands you'll stumble upon, or almost trip over,
the Peak District. It sits between Manchester and Sheffield,
Derby and Stoke on Trent. It's surrounded by England's greatest
cities and yet manages to remain wild and free, ripe for trespass
and tramping, despite the presence of industries long gone. Stick
around for a few days and you'll discover beautiful dales, caves,
peaks and lovely country towns. And a pass or two to
test the brakes. Give it a go.

DOVEDALE CAVES

BUXTON

A6    BASLOW    A619    A61

CHESTERFIELD

CHATSWORTH HOUSE

BAKEWELL

DERBYSHIRE

MATLOCK

A53

A615

A523

A515    B5056    A6

STEPPING STONES    TISSINGTON    CARSINGTON RESERVOIR

A520    A52    BELPER

ASHBOURNE    A517

A522    B5032    A515    A52

A50    ROCESTER    DERBY

UTTOXETER

A518    A50

A38

# ROUTE 13

# THE WHITE PEAK

## A NIGHT IN THE PUB

As National Parks go, the Peak District is the daddy. Not because of its size but because of its historical importance as the first to be created and the site of the first mass trespass, on Kinder Scout, in 1932. It sits at the heart of England, between some of the great northern conurbations. To the north lie Bradford, Huddersfield and Leeds, to the west, Manchester and Stockport, to the east, Sheffield and Chesterfield, and to the south, Buxton and Derby. It is surrounded by cities and yet remains a precious, protected place.

BEST FOR:
**Pub camping, walking, puddings and country houses**

START:
**Chatsworth**

END: **Uttoxeter**

MILEAGE: **66 miles (107 kilometres)**

DAYS TO EXPLORE: **2/3**

OS LANDRANGER MAP: **119**

175

**WhatsApp is going bananas.** My phone is pinging like mad with notifications from The Family, who are meeting up in an isolated pub somewhere nearby. We're on our way to that pub, near Biggin, where, we understand, lunch awaits us. We are due to meet at a car park in Hartington from where we will set off on the Tissington Trail, a disused railway line, for the pub.

We're a bit late so we're in a bit of a panic, trying to find our way to the A5012 from the A6, which runs from Derby to Stockport. We take a wrong turn just outside Matlock and end up retracing our steps. Now we're really late. Ping goes the phone, informing us that it's started snowing. We find our way and begin to climb out of Matlock on the Via Gellia road, a route that

follows a steep-sided wooded valley. The road twists and turns and it feels more like we're travelling along a gorge than a valley. It reminds me of roads I have driven on in the Picos de Europa in Spain. Except, of course, it's much, much colder. As we ascend, snowflakes begin to land on the windscreen. They are big and plump and it looks like they are going to stick around. For the time being the road is clear, but the further we go, the more the snow is settling. We slow down and drive on cautiously. By the time we arrive at the top of the valley, back in open country, the road is white and the flakes are less flake-like and more like dollops. It's almost a whiteout. I drive onwards, ever more slowly, aware that the motorhome I am driving, a Benimar, isn't mine and would be very expensive to replace or fix if I drifted into a ditch. We drop down the gears and crawl along. Meanwhile my phone is pinging away. Liz checks the messages and reads them to me as they come in: the car park is too snowy to get into; Anthea is stuck; Katie has skidded all over the place. It sounds like they are having trouble at the agreed meeting place, so we look at the map again to see what we could do instead.

The further we go, the heavier the snow. It's now an inch or so thick on the road and we are making new tracks. We are the only vehicle to have passed this way recently. To be honest, I am starting to worry a little. We arrive at the junction with the A515, the main trunk road between Ashbourne and Buxton. It's still snowing, but at least here there are tyre tracks in the snow. We take a left, opting to head for the pub rather than the car park where we had planned to meet first. We shall have to forgo the walk. Shame, in this weather. We round a corner and find cars blocking the road. We stop. Ahead of us is a hill where a number of cars are slipping and sliding as they attempt to get up it. A couple of them have pulled over, their occupants perhaps deciding what to do. One of the cars that's blocking our path does a very slow three-point turn in the road and trundles off back down the way we've just come.

We consider our options. We can leave the van here and walk to the pub. We can carry on. We can turn back. We can park up and stick the kettle on.

All but one of the vehicles attempting to make the climb fail and slide back down again or come to a stop before trying again. The only one that makes it is a Land Rover Discovery that's come out of a side road. It crawls up without a slip or a slide, making a mockery of the two-wheel drive vehicles around it.

We realise that the right turn, which is at the foot of the hill, is the turn we want, so we overtake the stopped vehicles and take the turn. The road is flat, thankfully. The snow here is already really deep – about 5 to 10cm (2 to 4in) – so we drive really slowly. It looks like the road heads off down a steep hill, but before it does, we come to the Waterloo Inn. We park up, put on our snow clothes and go to see if the pub is open. We meet the manager, who is attempting to clear the snow from the car park. We ask him if they are still doing lunch and if we'd be OK to stay overnight. He says it's no problem as they have a campsite at the back of the pub and everyone is currently packing up to leave. This is brilliant news, so we book in and wander round the back to the campsite to find a pitch. We notice that all the vehicles on the site are Land Rovers. It seems as if they've had a bit of a convention but are packing up in anticipation of worse snow to come! Ha!

We find a pitch we can get into without churning up the grass or getting stuck, plug into the electric, put the heating on and stroll off to the pub to await the rest of the family.

We're happy. It's a perfect outcome. We go in and order a pint or two. Whether we like it or not, we're here for the next day or so. Could be worse.

# THE DRIVING

This route is a little convoluted. But bear with me, because we'll see some nice stuff along the way! The reason it's so complicated is that we had such a nice time in the Peaks that we drove all over in a zigzag, enjoying the views and the roads and the countryside. However, the snow thwarted us at Biggin (see above), so we ended up taking all kinds of routes. We began at Chatsworth House, at the very excellent Caravan and Motorhome Club Site in the grounds. This is very special, and it is also handy for a late-night cycle down a very dark access road to the local pub, the Devonshire Arms at Baslow.

So, start at Chatsworth and head west on the B6048 and then the A619 to Bakewell. Stop here for an official Bakewell Pudding (*not* a tart, as you may think...) and then head north-west on the busy but winding A6 to Buxton. Once in Buxton, take the A515 to Ashbourne. This road has long, straight stretches and passes over high open countryside and farmland, with the occasional wood on either side. It will take you into Ashbourne, where you'll need to take a left for Belper and pick up the A6 north towards Matlock. At Cromford take the A5012, the Via Gellia road, up the gorge

and out into open country. At the junction with the A515 (which you have already been past) take a left and then a right into Biggin just before the hill. This will take you to the Waterloo Inn! If you don't want to camp, continue on the A515 and then take the left turn at Tissington that is signposted to Dovedale. This will take you into the very lovely Dovedale and on to the very nicely laid-out and very well-presented village of Ilam and Ilam Park.

From here, if you are heading south, take the B5032, then the B5030 south from Ashbourne through Ellastone and Rocester. It's very pretty.

## PLACES TO STAY

**The Waterloo Inn and Camp Site**
Main Street, Biggin-by-Hartington, Buxton, SK17 0DH
**web:** www.waterlooinnbiggin.com
**email:** waterlooinnbiggin@yahoo.co.uk
**tel:** 01298 84284

**info:** *A nice and cosy pub with a handy campsite out the back.*

**Chatsworth Park Caravan Club Site**
Baslow, Bakewell, Derbyshire, DE45 1PN
**web:** www.caravanclub.co.uk
**tel:** 01246 582226

**info:** *A great site in a walled garden on a posh estate. Love it? Yeah!*

# IN THE AREA

**Dovedale**  This lovely National Trust–owned valley is a National Nature Reserve with an important ancient ash forest and wildflower-rich grassland. Great walking and brilliant caves.  • www.nationaltrust.org.uk/ilam-park-dovedale-and-the-white-peak

**Chatsworth House**  Home to the Duke and Duchess of Devonshire and their lovely gardens. Worth poking around in the artwork and antiques there for some real treasures. They've been renovating hard over the last few years and things are looking good, for a stately home. The café is ace. • www.chatsworth.org

**The Old Original Bakewell Pudding Shop**  Do not get this confection confused with a tart, never, no.  • www.bakewellpuddingshop.co.uk

**The Tissington Trail**  This is a 13-mile cycle/walking route that follows the old Buxton to Ashbourne railway. • www.sustrans.org.uk/ncn/map/route/tissington-trail

**Poole's Cavern, Buxton**
A proper show cave and country park. • www. poolescavern.co.uk

> **Nearest van hire**
>
> **Simply Cool Campers**
>  • www.simplycoolcampers.co.uk

Snake Pass
Summit 1680 feet

HUDDERSFIELD

M1

KIRKLEES

HOLMFIRTH

A635

A628

WOODHEAD

A616

MANCHESTER

B6105  BLEAKLOW
HILL

PEAK
DISTRICT

STOCKSBRIDGE

GLOSSOP

HOPE
FOREST

HOWDEN RESERVOIR

SNAKE PASS

A624

KINDER
SCOUT

A57

DERWENT RESERVOIR

SHEFFIELD

NEW
MILLS

HAYFIELD

LADYBOWER RESERVOIR

A6187

HOPE

A6013

BAMFORD

CHAPEL-EN-LE-FRITH

BLUE JOHN
CAVERN

HATHERSAGE

A6

A623

B6049

A625

BUXTON

A6

BLUE JOHN CAVERN

ROUTE 14

# DERWENT AND THE DARK PEAK

## THUNDERING PEAKS AND WATERFALLS

Under the Millstone Grit of the Dark Peak lie seams of precious metals and stones, while on the surface there are some classic high passes and gorges to drive. The Peaks might be between the conurbations and all the busier for it, but the scenery is lovely and the driving amazing.

BEST FOR:
**Caves, gorges, views**

START: **Hope**

END:
**Hathersage**

MILEAGE: **62 miles (100 kilometres)**

DAYS TO EXPLORE: **2/3**

OS LANDRANGER MAP: **110**

THE MIDLANDS

185

**How are you with enclosed spaces?** I'm not that great to be honest, but I am always willing to give it a go if there's the chance of a show cave with stalagmites and stalactites and some creative lighting to lift the mood out of the darkness. Ooohs and ahhhs are always welcome as they switch on the lights and illuminate some feature that looks a bit like someone famous (usually the Virgin Mary).

I like caves, but not small ones. I found this out while caving in the Dales a few years ago when I had to pour myself through a squeeze. With rising panic, I had to talk myself down as I wriggled through a gap the size of a sausage under thousands of tonnes or rock. I've not been into a cave since, despite my love of a good Victorian grotto adventure.

We're on our way to the Blue John Cavern over Winnats Pass from Hope Vale, the steep route that joins Chapel-en-le-Frith with Hathersage. To our right is Mam Tor and the old A625, a winding, less steep alternative

to Winnats Pass that was abandoned in 1979 due to constant landfalls. Winnats, as 'the old route', is the haunted road, passing through a steep limestone gorge where the wind, that gives the pass its name (it's a corruption of 'windy gates'), howls in mourning for the star-crossed lovers murdered by greedy miners in 1758. It took ten years for their bodies to be found in one of the limestone caves that permeate this landscape.

The Dark Peak is so called because its lighter limestone base is topped by Millstone Grit, a coarse

sandstone. Mam Tor, to our right, looks like a steep wave with a black crest about to tumble and slide into the valley below. The highest edges of the pass bear down on us, too, as we ascend. Dark towers of rock overhang the road as we snake our way up the gorge.

We take a right and follow the road to the Blue John Cavern, home to 'eight of the fourteen known varieties of Blue John stone, a beautiful and ornamental fluor-spar', or so the sign says. I am excited, of course, to have the chance to explore the caves, but we find we are thwarted by the weather. The caves are closed because they are flooded after the heavy snow the day before. It's warmed up quickly, causing meltwater to filter down through the limestone and into the caves. We turn around and make

our way back down the gorge to our second choice, Peak Cavern. It's also closed due to flooding, which forces us towards Speedwell Cavern, a disused lead mine and cave offering an incredible subterranean boat journey. It sounds good, so we pay our entrance fee, don our hard hats and descend 105 steps into the heart of the limestone. At the bottom we find a metal boat moored up at a landing stage. The water, so the guide tells us, is very high today, so we'd better watch our heads. We have to duck the whole way as the boat takes us along the underground canal. It's crushing being here, with the low ceiling bearing down upon us as we quietly move along the water. We hear how young boys were used to set dynamite to blast the rock and how miners followed seams of lead into the hillside. At the end of our journey we land at a natural cave, the Bottomless Pit, an underground lake that was backfilled using the rock from the mining and that is now just 11 metres (36ft) deep rather than bottomless. The water is very heavy here, with huge gushing waterfalls plunging into the Bottomless Pit. Above us another gaping hole in the rock spills tonnes of water into the pit. It's noisy, dark, spray filled and

oppressive and I can't wait to get to the surface. I feel as if the water, which is sloshing around my shoes, is rising all the time.

Back at the landing stage, I can't wait to stride up the 105 steps to the surface, but it's impossible to move quickly because of the roof height. It's a steady, shuffling plod, and then we're gulping lungfuls of sharp, cold air as the door opens to the world outside. We're out and it feels wonderful.

We drive on, back up the gorge and down into Chapel-en-le-Frith. Along the way we peer down into deep dales and see sheep grazing between perfect lines of dry-stone walls. It's a dark day in the Dark Peak. We look up at Kinder Scout from New Mills and thank the trespassers who took part in the 1932 act of mass civil disobedience for their efforts to make this land free for all, for the creation of the National Parks, for open access.

We head into Glossop and then take the beautiful back road up to the Woodhead Pass, which we follow to its apex above the Woodhead Reservoir. It's busy with dirty, thundering traffic – not our idea of perfect Peaks. We retrace our steps and make our way along the A57 to Derwent Dale and the Derwent Reservoir, where we walk to the wall of water that's thundering over Howden Dam. It's 100 feet wide and over a hundred feet tall, so it looks like a breaking tsunami above our heads. I take pictures in the mist, loving the way the dam creates a solid backdrop, overshadows the trees and shrouds us in spray. It's moody, dark and dangerous. But we love it.

# THE DRIVING

This route is more of a meandering than an A to B. We began at Hope (why not? It's the very best starting point for any adventure, even here), at the Castleton Caravan and Motorhome Club Site. Heading west, we followed the A6187 up to Speedwell Cavern and up Winnats Pass, with a short detour up the old A625 towards Mam Tor. The views from here are lovely and there is some good walking. From Winnats Pass we took a right towards the top of the old A625 and the Blue John Cavern, which took us to Chapel-en-le-Frith via Rushup Edge. We avoided the A6 at Chapel-en-le-Frith, instead taking the stunning A624 towards Hayfield and Glossop. This road takes you up to the lovely pass overlooked by Kinder Scout, an imposing presence above Hayfield. From there we followed the A624 north into Glossop, exiting the town on the B6105, which twists and turns its way to the Woodhead Reservoir, crossing between Woodhead and Rhodeswood reservoirs before joining the A628 Woodhead Pass. It's a great road, but, as one of the main crossing points between Manchester and Sheffield, it's busy with heavy traffic. Worth a look, but still very busy.

We headed back along the B6105 and took the A57 (Snake Pass) from Glossop. It's a much nicer road than the Woodhead Pass, although still busy. It snakes up out of Glossop following the course of the Hurst Brook past the Hurst Reservoir and up to the watershed at 510m (1,706ft) above sea level. The descent to Ladybower Reservoir is lovely, with a lot of this through woodland. The road follows the River Ashop as it meanders into the reservoir. A left turn here takes you up past Derwent Reservoir and up to Howden Dam. Back on the A57 (here known as Snake Road), a right turn at the junction with the A6013 takes you into the lovely town of Hathersage, home of Alpkit, the lovely Hathersage Swimming Pool (outdoor swimming) and also a wonderful greengrocer!

## PLACES TO STAY

**Castleton Caravan Club Site**
Castleton, Derbyshire, S33 8WB
**web:** www.caravanclub.co.uk
**tel:** 01433 620636

**info:** *Another tidy, friendly club site.*

**Upper Booth Farm & Campsite**
Edale, Hope Valley, Derbyshire S33 7ZJ
**web:** www.upperboothcamping.co.uk
**tel:** 01433 670250
**email:** mail@helliwell.info

**info:** *No Wi-Fi, virtually no phone signal, no fires, no big campers (small ones welcome in summer). Apart from that, idyllic.*

# IN THE AREA

**Speedwell Cavern** Speedwell and Peak Caverns offer 2 for 1 on underground adventures ... show caves! ▪ www.speedwellcavern.co.uk

**Hathersage Pool** Amazingly lovely outdoor pool. ▪ www. hathersageswimmingpool.co.uk

**Derwent Reservoir** Walking trails, cycling and café. ▪ www.visitpeakdistrict.com/visitor-information/upper-derwent-visitor-centre-p681481

**Kinder Scout** A trail that follows in the footsteps of the original ramblers. ▪ www.nationaltrust.org.uk/kinder-edale-and-the-dark-peak/trails/kinder-scout-mass-trespass-walk

**The Blue John Cavern** Natural, water-worn caverns and mine workings. ▪ www.bluejohn-cavern.co.uk

**Cycling** Peak District off-road cycling is said to be fantastic! On yer bike... ▪ www.peakdistrict.gov. uk/visiting/cycle/cycle-routes

Nearest van hire

**Peaks and Dales Motorhome Hire** ▪ www.peaksanddalesmotor homehire.com

**WALES**

I could have written a whole book
on Wales – and probably should have, simply
because there is so much of it that's amazing. Driving from
south to north takes you to some wonderful places: independently
minded towns, a National Park, mountains and lakes. Head west
and you'll discover secret swimming spots in the hills, narrow-gauge
railways and wonky bridges. Head to the far west and follow the bus
on a rollercoaster ride through Pembrokeshire's loveliest coastal
scenery. There, near Britain's smallest city, you'll find
glorious beaches, great campsites and a whole
new way to see the coast.

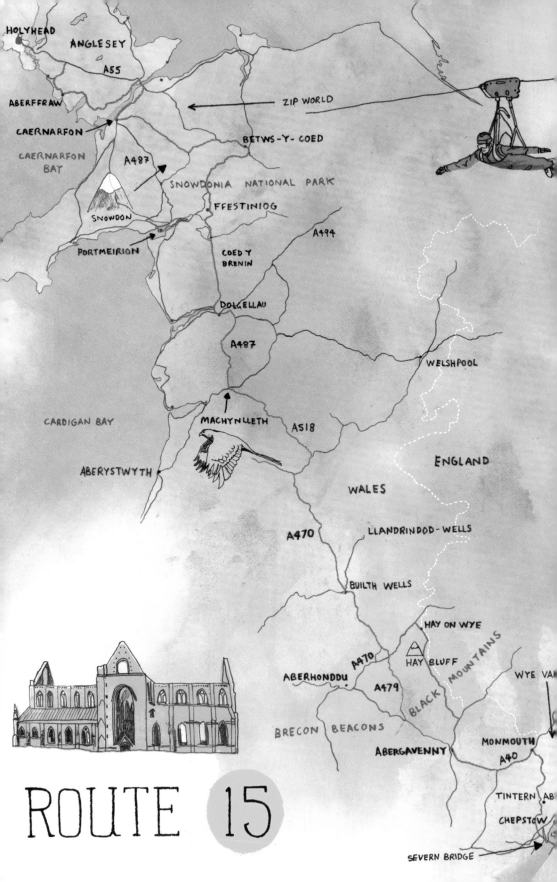

HOLYHEAD

ANGLESEY

A55

ZIP WORLD

ABERFFRAW

CAERNARFON

BETWS-Y-COED

CAERNARFON BAY

A487

SNOWDONIA NATIONAL PARK

FFESTINIOG

SNOWDON

A494

PORTMEIRION

COED Y BRENIN

DOLGELLAU

A487

WELSHPOOL

CARDIGAN BAY

MACHYNLLETH

A518

ENGLAND

WALES

ABERYSTWYTH

LLANDRINDOD-WELLS

A470

BUILTH WELLS

HAY ON WYE

HAY BLUFF

ABERHONDDU

A470

WYE VAL

A479

BLACK MOUNTAINS

BRECON BEACONS

MONMOUTH

A40

ABERGAVENNY

TINTERN AB

CHEPSTOW

ROUTE 15

SEVERN BRIDGE

# 15

# WALES COAST TO COAST

## SHORTCUTS AND SLOW ROADS

If you draw a straight(ish) line between Bristol and Holyhead you'll find a route that will lead you on a merry dance through central and North Wales via some of its loveliest roads, a very high pass and a couple of lovely lakes. You'll pass Snowdon too, so don't be afraid to stop and climb. It's lovely.

This route is a long-distance journey that will take you to some of the best of Wales. If you are heading for Holyhead it's much nicer than taking the M5, then the M52 to Shrewsbury or the M6 and then M56 to Runcorn. And it'll take you just about the same time.

**BEST FOR:**
High passes, mountains, lakes

**START:** Bristol

**END:** Holyhead

**MILEAGE: 244** miles (392 kilometres)

**DAYS TO EXPLORE: 4**

**OS LANDRANGER MAP: 172, 162, 161, 147, 136, 124, 115, 114**

WALES

197

Section I

# BRISTOL TO MONMOUTH

We're searching for wild garlic. That's today's mission because I have to write a piece about making wild garlic pesto and I haven't had time to search for some before we leave for Holyhead. It grows in abundance near home, but I didn't have time to pick some before we left. So now we're looking out for it, but I am beginning to worry a little that I am too late or that we'll drive right past it.

We drove over the old Severn suspension bridge – because we're in no hurry – and made our way towards the Wye Valley. Almost immediately the scenery is stunning and we're winding around bends and following the course of this meandering body of water to our right.

We round a bend and there, facing us, is the impressive ruin of Tintern Abbey. We pull in to the car park to take some pictures and enjoy what many have enjoyed, written about and painted before. We walk between the abbey and the river, looking for greenery good enough to garnish some

# HAY-ON-WYE TO MACHYNLLETH

It's always a thrill to reach Llanidloes and take the right over the bridge, and then turn left. It feels a little too normal and everyday to be taking you somewhere special as you drive between the houses and up and out of town, but that soon changes. With the new Red Kite Touring Park to your left on the valley side below you, you start to climb out of the treeline and into the hills.

I have driven this road many times, as it cuts off a corner of the A470, but still it's exciting to soar out of town and into the wide-open spaces. The reveal of Clywedog reservoir is always a thrill and always causes us to stop at the car park overlooking it. We pull in and get out of the van to admire the view. Below us we see the reservoir, the dam to the right and the sailing club opposite. Wooded slopes jut out into the water: it looks like a great place to explore. In the distance a sailing boat catches the breeze.

From the reservoir it's an uphill climb and then a left towards Machynlleth for the final flourish before the cruise into town. If you drive just one road in Wales this year, make it this one.

We arrive at the top, with the descent ahead of us, and stop. Below us is another stunning view – one of the best in Wales, possibly – towards the coast. From our position, perched on the edge of a big drop, we can see mountains in the distance and fields and forest between. While the grass and bracken are yellowed, having died back over winter, the view is a kaleidoscope of greens, from dark plantations to light, fresh spring growth. It's vast, wide open and lung-bustingly lovely. We gulp in the ozone, drink it all in and prepare to move on. It'll be hard to beat.

# THE DRIVING

The A470 is the main road that you'll have to take if you want to bisect Wales from north to south. To get to it from Hay-on-Wye you need to take the A438 south for a few miles. Then, take a right-hand turn, the A479, signposted to Builth Wells. At Llyswen it turns into the A470 and continues up the beautiful Wye Valley to Builth Wells and beyond. It's a lovely stretch of road that's close to the southern shore of the Wye River.

The road follows the Wye even further past Builth Wells through Rhayader and as far as Llangurig, when it makes a move to the north-west and crosses over into the Severn Valley at Llanidloes. It is here that you need to be vigilant or you'll miss the turn-off for the B4518. On the bypass, take a left towards Llanidloes, take a right over the river and then take a left through the houses, following brown signs for Llyn Clywedog. It's then uphill to the lake, and out on to open country. A little way past the lake, there is a small left turn that is signposted to Machynlleth which will take you out on to the mountain road and then down the lush, winding valley into the town.

# PLACES TO STAY

**Red Kite Touring Park**
Van Road, Llanidloes, Powys, Mid Wales, SY18 6NG
**web:** www.redkitetouringpark.co.uk
**email:** info@redkitetouringpark.co.uk
**tel:** 01686 412122

**info:** *An adults-only site in a great position on the edge of town and edge of the moor. Great for exploring high places.*

Section 4

# MACHYNLLETH TO BANGOR

We're kitted out: red boiler suits, helmets, goggles and harnesses that trail behind us as we walk, clanking like climbers with too much clobber on. Charlie, the girl who hates roller coasters, is looking a bit worried. I reassure her that things will work out, but I'm having trouble hiding my own anxiety. The truth is that I'm no good with heights, so this latest adventure, taking Europe's longest zip line across a quarry in North Wales, is starting to look a little like folly.

Maggie is more optimistic. She's looking excited about flying down a wire at 100 miles per hour. I hold Charlie's hand as we walk out of the Portakabin containing racks and racks of more red boiler suits and helmets. We clank along to the first of two zip lines, the Little Zipper, a short warm-up zip that takes us over the road and trees to the take-off zone for Velocity, the big one.

There are two wires side by side, so Maggie goes first, followed by me and Charlie. It's not so scary at all. We are harnessed from behind so we

lie face down, looking straight down at the ground, which is only a few feet away at the start. It's a lovely ride, almost through the canopy of the trees, alongside the quarry lake and then a blunt stop across the water. Easy.

We clamber aboard an old troop-carrying red truck for the ride to the start of Velocity, the big one. We expect the journey to be over in a few minutes, but it takes 20 minutes of driving up and around the mountain on twisting quarry roads. The views get better and better the more we climb until we reach the very top of the mountain. There, at the head of a man-made gorge, is the start of Velocity, the big one. We look down. Below us are the turquoise blue lake and the terraces of the quarry that was once the world biggest. It's 1,200 feet (366m) deep and a mile across. Beyond that we see Bethesda, and beyond that the sea.

Suddenly I realise that we are very high up and that I am about to send my children down a zip line that's a mile long and that will send them into the abyss at speeds of up to 100mph. I can't even see the end of the pair of wires. We look at the people before us in the queue. They lie face down while the attendants count down from three before releasing them into the blue. There is a clank and then they are gone, screaming as they go.

I have a dilemma. There are two wires but three of us. What do I do?

If I go down with Charlie it'll leave Maggie all alone at the top. If I send her first it'll leave her alone at the bottom. If I go down first it'll leave both the girls at the top. What if Charlie decides not to go once I've gone? There is only one answer: they'll have to go down first and keep each other company at the bottom.

The wait is interminable. Someone has got stuck halfway down and has had to be rescued. They tell me this has to be done by someone at the bottom who will shimmy out in a special harness. It happens from time to time if you don't go fast enough.

Then at last it's our turn. They call out the countdown and Maggie and Charlie look at me with thumbs up. Three. Two. One. Clank. And they are gone. I follow them as much as I can, but after a while they disappear from view. Then it's my turn. I get clipped in and lie face down, looking at the quarry fade away from me in the distance. It takes an age. Then I hear there has been a delay. I wait. Radios buzz around me. Time marches on

and I begin to get nervous. What if something has happened to the girls? I begin to think the worst. I'm hanging there, unable to move, with my arms strapped beside me, and there's nothing I can do.

Finally, it's three, two, one and I am off down the wire. The ground races as the wire follows the gorge down the mountain, then it feels as if I have slowed right down as I whoosh out over the water and the ground drops away. It's hard to tell how fast I am going now I have no point of reference, but I know that I am going very, very fast as my cheeks are rippling and my eyes are watering beneath my goggles. Then I see the end of the wire and I realise I need to slow myself down by opening my arms into a swallow dive. And then it's coming up really fast now. I hit the stopper and crash to a halt, swinging for a moment before being released so I can walk away. I see the girls waiting for me. Thank goodness. I walk over.

'All right?' I ask.

'Yes,' they reply. 'Can we do it again?'

# THE DRIVING

The mountain road from Llyn Clywedog joins the A489 just outside Machynlleth and then joins the A487 in a T-junction in this jolly antique-shop- and hippy-filled town. Turn right here and head north out of town and into beautiful dramatic countryside. At the River Dovey turn right over the old bridge and then follow a tributary up a narrow, twisting valley past the Centre for Alternative Technology. Further

on, after Corris, you enter the gorgeous Cwmrhwyddfor, a long, steep and straight valley heading inland with the mighty Cadair Idris on its northern side. Don't forget to turn around and look at the views towards Towyn and the coast. At the Cross Foxes Inn you'll rejoin the A470 and follow it past Dolgellau and up to Llyn Trawsfynydd and the rather monolithic nuclear power station (swim, anyone?). Then take a right (still following the A470) up to Blaenau Ffestiniog. The landscape changes greatly here as you enter a North Wales that's very different from the green valleys you've just come through. The town itself is post-industrial, with much of it seeming to merge in with the slate quarries. The road takes you right through the centre of town, past the quarries and huge piles of waste slate. Almost as quickly as it changed it changes back again into a bucolic breeze of a landscape as the A470 rumbles on towards Betws-y-Coed and the A5 on the banks of the River Conwy. The A5 is the main road through North Wales, but even so, it's still a difficult, winding affair that hits open country outside Capel Curig before making a dog leg to the north at the lovely Llyn Ogwen, squeezing through Bethesda and then plonking itself firmly at the A55 just outside Bangor, giving you the feeling that you've just been through something truly special. And you have. Only a diversion to the west, via the Llanberis Pass, could be better, but if you're planning on heading back in that direction I'd go for it. Well worth the view from the top of the pass – although get there early if you want to climb Snowdon, as the car park gets full quickly.

# IN THE AREA

There is so much to do in Wales, particularly in North Wales, as it has recently become the self-styled 'adventure capital' of the UK. There is certainly a lot of fun to be had, from surfing on an artificial lake to whizzing down a mountain on a skeleton bob thing. It's all there.

**Zip World**  Zip World has it all at three different locations across North Wales: a wild ride down a mountain at speeds of god knows what, zip lines in a tree canopy, zip lines in a disused slate cavern, a via ferrata inside a slate cavern and trampolines inside a slate cavern. Take your pick. All amazing.
  ▪ www.zipworld.co.uk

**Surf Snowdonia**  Anyone can have a go at this, the world's first public-access surfing lake. It looks mighty fun.  ▪ www.surfsnowdonia.com

**Centre for Alternative Technology**  If you want to know the future, better book a day out and go here. All kinds of eco brilliance and ideas to inspire you!  ▪ www.cat.org.uk

## PLACES TO STAY

**Gwern Gof Uchaf**
Capel Curig, Betws-y-Coed, Snowdonia, North Wales, LL24 0EU
**web:** www.tryfanwales.co.uk
**tel:** 01690 720294

**info:** *A small campsite on the A5 that's handy for all attractions and local walking.*

**Mountain Biking at Coed y Brenin**  A beautifully situated centre with plenty of opportunities for biking in the forest, no matter what your ability is. Lovely eco building near Machynlleth.

• www.mbwales.com/agents/coed-y-brenin

**Slate Caverns**  It was a tough life in the caverns for the quarrymen living and working in Blaenau Ffestiniog. This tour of the caverns, using the original train, is fascinating. Deep stuff from a very deep mine.

• www.llechwedd-slate-caverns.co.uk

**Snowdon**  Wales and England's highest peak is one of the area's biggest draws, attracting thousands of visitors. You can walk up and down or you can take the train up from Llanberis or back down to Llanberis. There are various ways up to the peak, the most popular of which is the Miners' Track from Pen-y-Pass at the head of the Llanberis Pass.

• www. snowdonrailway.co.uk

Nearest van hire

**Taffi Campers**
• www.tafficampers.co.uk

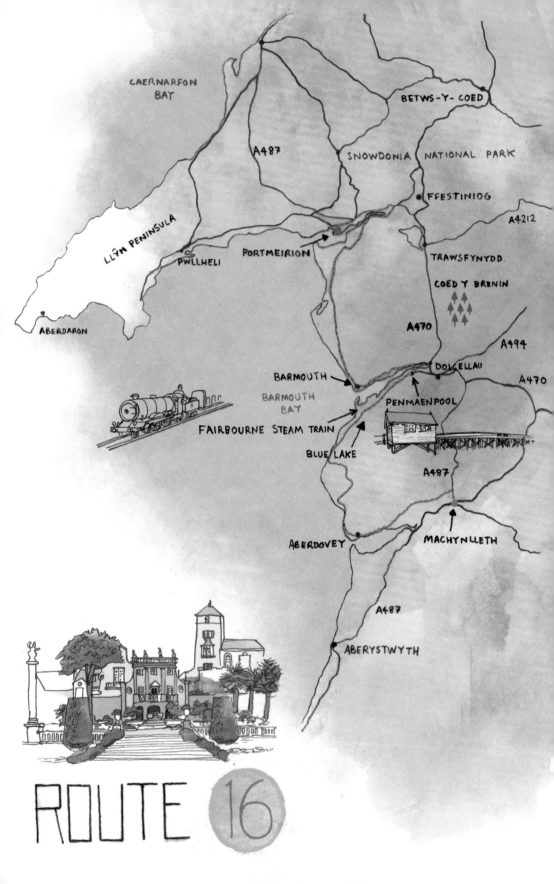

CAERNARFON BAY

BETWS-Y-COED

A487

SNOWDONIA NATIONAL PARK

FFESTINIOG

A4212

LLŶN PENINSULA

PWLLHELI

PORTMEIRION

TRAWSFYNYDD

COED Y BRENIN

ABERDARON

A470

A494

DOLGELLAU

A470

BARMOUTH

BARMOUTH BAY

PENMAENPOOL

FAIRBOURNE STEAM TRAIN

BLUE LAKE

A487

A487

ABERDOVEY

MACHYNLLETH

A487

ABERYSTWYTH

ROUTE 16

# WEST WALES

## WILD SWIMS IN THE HILLS

The west coast of Wales is an absolute gem, with a little of everything for everybody. In fact, taking a drive from Aberdovey to Portmeirion was the journey that triggered this whole 'slow road' idea. So it's the original and best, a journey of pootles and dawdles that never fails to deliver.

BEST FOR: Wild swimming, walking, riding trains

START: Machynlleth

END: Portmeirion

MILEAGE: 47 miles (76 kilometres)

DAYS TO EXPLORE: 2

OS LANDRANGER MAP: 135, 124

WALES

It's not easy finding the way to the Blue Lake. But persevere we must. We park near the railway station and walk up the A493 for a few hundred yards until we find the no-through road, a narrow lane that slowly works its way past a few cottages alongside a narrow brook. It's wooded and shadowed as we walk in the dappled afternoon sun. There is a faint whiff of wild garlic from the shaded banks. At a fork in the road we take a right-hand turn up a steep pathway. It leads us up into the hillside along a damp and slippery path, past old mining ruins and up to a man-made plateau. We arrive at a disused quarry, a post-industrial landscape high above the main road below. We look down and see Barmouth to the north and the coast at Fairbourne to the west.

The Blue Lake that we are searching for is a secret body of water somewhere in this quarry that's said to be 'bottomless' and yet incredibly clear, with visibility of about 5–6m (16–19ft). It's an abandoned hydro-electric scheme and is a little-known wild swimming spot. There isn't much information on the internet about the lake so I am following my nose, on a whim, because I like the idea of swimming

in a bottomless pit that's azure blue, regardless of the weather.

We wander around this plateau for a little while, searching for the entrance to the lake, a wet and low tunnel in the hillside. We have no idea what to expect or where it might be, but we do find it and make our way through, using old slabs of slate as stepping stones to cross wide, ankle-deep pools on the floor of the tunnel. It's an uncomfortable stoop, but it's only 25m (82ft) to the bright sunshine beyond. There is a choice of a right or left fork, so we take the right and come out at the lakeside.

Standing up straight, I look around. I am in a crucible of rock with high, sheer sides of 5 to 10 metres (16–32ft) rising up all around. There is a narrow pathway leading left and right, skirting the lake, a slope of quarry spoil to my right and a sheer wall dropping into the water opposite. The lake is blue, so impossibly blue, and clear. But I can't see the bottom, only the straight-down sides of the quarry as they disappear into the depths.

There are some swimmers here already, a group of teenagers, who have taken up residence on the left bank. We take the right, rushing to get out of our clothes and into our wetsuits. There is a shallow shelf on our side, so we can wade into the water for a few feet before committing to the plunge. The water is clear and it's windless in the shelter of the quarry walls. I jump. It's cool, and when I open my eyes underwater I can see the bubbles I have made in extraordinary detail. I can see well beyond my feet, and yet I see nothing below. It's not a gloom that I have to penetrate, just a distance that I can't see an end of. The idea is frightening. What lies below? What if I were to sink? All those casual what-ifs that come with swimming in deep open water come to me in the moment before I bob up. I shake myself out of it and remember that my wetsuit will keep me afloat so there is no chance of sinking into the abyss this time.

In reality the Blue Lake is only 12m (39ft) deep. Deep enough. I come to the surface and look around. My girls leap from a rock a few metres above the surface, screaming with abandon as they plunge into the water, laughing as they come up into the hot and still summer air. A leap into the unknown, a secret swimming spot – a perfect way to spend a lazy summer afternoon.

# THE DRIVING

The A487 takes you out of Machynlleth north, past the station and along the top end of the Dyfi Valley. Here you'll meet the old stone bridge at the river, where you'll need to take a left turn to follow the course of the river down towards the coast and Aberdovey. While the river meanders the road takes a higher course towards Pennal before they converge again, this time with the railway too, a few miles downstream. The road then follows the northern bank of the estuary into Aberdovey, giving wonderful views over the water to the south. The ride into Aberdovey is sensational too, as you pass Victorian seafront houses with that unmistakable nautical elegance that comes from occupying a prime position on the quayside. Stop here, for sure, to try crabbing or seafood, or for a wander round the quirky shops. Get crab bait from the shop on the quayside.

The A493 continues out of Aberdovey, past the golf club and dunes, and heads a little inland before coming to Tywyn, a completely different kind of place. A detour to the seafront reveals soulless caravan parks and a mix of architecture, from new-town 1970s-style blocks to terraces of Victorian B&Bs. After Tywyn the road turns inland again to allow for the estuarine sands of the Dysynni estuary. Once over the river, the road creeps upwards to pop over the hills, with a sharp right-hand turn at the Cae Du campsite revealing one of the loveliest stretches of coast road anywhere.

With craggy, fern-covered hills to your right and the glorious Irish Sea to your left this is one hell of a road. The railways runs below it for most of this stretch, with a few farms on the seaward side. Stone walls run across green fields down to the sea. The views are amazing, with the Llŷn Peninsula visible on clear days. There are a few caravan parks along this stretch too, at the lovely village of Llwyngwril. The point on which the caravan site is situated, on its day, produces excellent waves. Further on, as you approach the beach at Fairbourne, the road and railway are compressed into a narrow strip between hills and sea. And then you drop into Fairbourne and the Mawddach estuary at Barmouth, heading away up the river and away from the coast to the nearest crossing point.

You can cross the river at the rickety wooden bridge at Penmaenpool, but only if you're small enough and light enough to cross. It costs one pound for motorhomes.

If you don't want to chance your arm, or they won't let you cross, then you'll have to make your way upstream another few miles to the A470 at Dolgellau before picking up the A496 again for the run into jolly, bright and breezy, fish-and-chip-happy Barmouth. The beach here is fantastic, and it's worth another stop, if only for a bag of chips on the seafront or a stroll over the estuary on the railway bridge.

After Barmouth it's another coastal jaunt before the road goes inland behind Shell Island and the airstrip at Llanbedr on its way to Harlech and another wide estuary. As you round the bend you see the mountains of Snowdonia brooding in the distance, with the spine of North Wales stretching off to the west and the Llŷn Peninsula. Follow the road over the Pont Briwet bridge for the final leg into Porthmadog, but don't be tempted to take the bypass: the old main road will take you to Portmeirion and alongside the steam railway and along the causeway. It's a much more interesting drive with great views.

## PLACES TO STAY

**Cae Du Campsite**
Rhosllefain, Tywyn, Gwynedd, LL36 9ND
**web:** www.caedufarmholidays.co.uk
**tel:** 01654 711234
**email:** info@caedufarmholidays.co.uk

**info:** *Open fires, friendly farmer and amazing location.*

**Nyth Robin Campsite**
Panteidal, Aberdovey, Gwynedd, LL35 ORG
**web:** www.nythrobin.co.uk
**tel:** 07731 783534

**info:** *Quiet and secluded yet conveniently on the main road, and good clean facilities.*

**Shell Island Campsite**
Shell Island Llanbedr, Gwynedd,
North Wales, LL45 2PJ
**web:** www.shellisland.co.uk
**tel:** 01341 241453

**info:** *One of Europe's biggest campsites, with 300 acres of camping. About as wild as it gets, if you can find a spot in the dunes to yourselves.*

# IN THE AREA

**Fairbourne Narrow Gauge Steam Railway**  A cute narrow-gauge railway which runs from the station at Fairbourne to the ferry at Fairbourne Point. You could walk it quicker, but that's not the point.
• www.fairbournerailway.com

**Barmouth Ferry**  The ferry usually runs from Easter to the end of October, connecting with trains from Fairbourne, and takes visitors across the estuary from Barmouth to Penrhyn Point on the opposite bank.

**The Mawddach Trail**  A 15km walking trail from Barmouth to Dolgellau along disused railway lines.  • www.mawddachtrail.co.uk

**The Blue Lake**  Find it if you can. Near Fairbourne.

**Portmeirion**  The Italianate village that's very pretty but still trading on a 1960s TV show ... lovely, though!
• www.portmeirion.wales

**Nearest van hire**

**Snowdonia Classic Campers**
• www.snowdoniaclassiccampers.co.uk

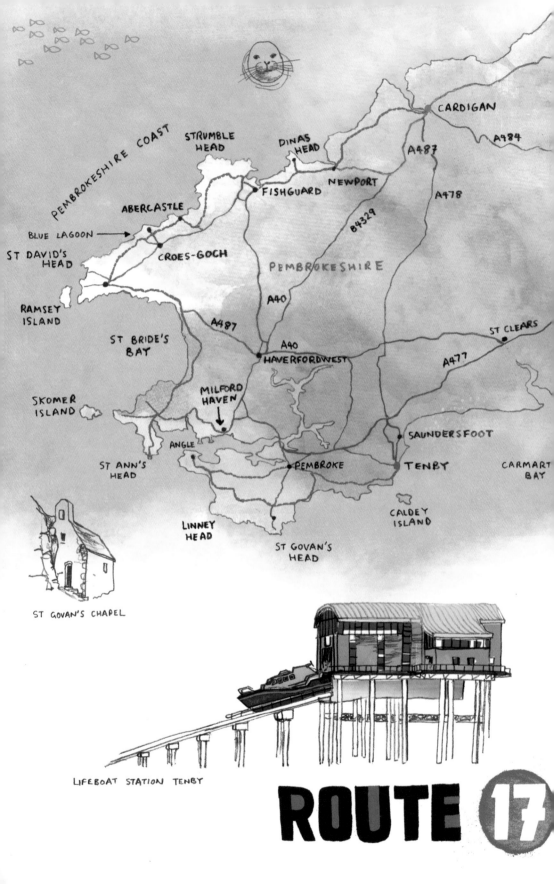

PEMBROKESHIRE COAST

CARDIGAN

STRUMBLE HEAD

DINAS HEAD

A984

A487

NEWPORT

A478

FISHGUARD

ABERCASTLE

B4329

BLUE LAGOON

PEMBROKESHIRE

ST DAVID'S HEAD

CROES-GOCH

A40

RAMSEY ISLAND

A487

ST BRIDE'S BAY

A40

ST CLEARS

HAVERFORDWEST

A477

SKOMER ISLAND

MILFORD HAVEN

SAUNDERSFOOT

ANGLE

ST ANN'S HEAD

PEMBROKE

TENBY

CARMART BAY

CALDEY ISLAND

LINNEY HEAD

ST GOVAN'S HEAD

ST GOVAN'S CHAPEL

LIFEBOAT STATION TENBY

# ROUTE 17

# THE PEMBROKE-SHIRE COAST NATIONAL PARK

## THE POPPIT ROCKET ...
## AND BEYOND

This route is an epic dawdle, a most excellent meander, a paragon of pootling. It has just about everything a slow road adventurer could ask for, and then some. Based on the alluringly named bus routes that serve the Pembrokeshire Coast National Park, this generally gentle – though sometimes challenging – amble will take you to lighthouses, beaches, castles, beaches, a cathedral city, beaches, inlets, beaches, wild swimming spots and some more beaches. And then, if you haven't had enough of the beaches, there's a beach that's been named as 'one of the world's best'.

BEST FOR:
**Coastline, done right**

START:
**Cardigan**

END: **Tenby**

MILEAGE: **125 miles (201 kilometres)**

DAYS TO EXPLORE: **4**

OS LANDRANGER MAP: **145, 157, 158**

WALES

**We are woken by excited voices** outside the van. I look at my watch. It's eight o'clock and we've been asleep for about an hour and a half. We arrived here, at Abereiddy, at about six thirty after an overnight drive, with a brief stop to snooze outside Carmarthen. We came here to swim in the Blue Lagoon, a breached, disused slate quarry and favourite spot on the Pembrokeshire coast between St David's and Fishguard. The idea was that we'd arrive before anyone else, swim, then tootle up the coast on the main road, the A487, to Cardigan to begin the route proper. When we arrived it was drizzling and windy and the lagoon didn't look so inviting so we went back to bed.

I look out of the window to see where the talking is coming from. I can see that the car park is now full (where before there were just a few campers), and there are people everywhere getting changed into swimming

wetsuits. A dinghy is towing three huge yellow buoys out into the bay. I get out and ask someone what's going on. I hear that today is the day of the Monster Swim, a 2.5-mile (4km) crawl that finishes up in the Blue Lagoon. Oh well. There will be no swimming there today then.

Still, no matter. We have a lot of coastline to cover and a lot of things to see and do. We pack up breakfast, put the van in gear and hit the road. As the swimmers take to the water a rainbow arcs across the sea. It's a sign that it's going to be a good, possibly mixed, day.

We pick up the route of the Poppit Rocket, the 405 bus that follows the coast from Cardigan to Fishguard, at the bridge over the River Teifi at Cardigan. Heading up the hill, we cruise through St Dogmaels and along

the river before landing at Poppit Sands, a wide stretch of beach and dunes at the estuary. It's Sunday and there are a lot of people enjoying this last day of August. We resist a cup of tea in the café and continue on up the hill and away from the beach, into the coastal countryside where late-blooming toadflax and evening primrose add splashes of yellow to the hedgerows.

A lunch stop brings us to Newport Sands, where we park adjacent to the beach. We could have parked right on the sand (take note), but it costs extra (take extra note). We pay for an hour and make a picnic in the van.

Scanning the beach, Liz notices an elderly lady at the far end strip off her top half and march down to the water's edge. 'She's brave,' she says, thinking more of the exposure than of the water temperature, I'm sure. The lady swims for a while, a source of fascination for some of the beachgoers (and us) with her apparent lack of regard for British respectability and sensibilities, before scampering out of the water to her towel, arms across her chest – as if her top had come off in the water. It seems a little paradoxical.

We watch, fascinated and a little bemused, and chuckle to ourselves as she opens her arms to bare all with a carefree flourish before putting on her T-shirt. It's an act that says, 'So what? It's a sunny Sunday in Wales and I don't care!' Good for her, we think. We dare to skinny-dip only where no one can see.

After Fishguard we drive up to Strumble Head, on the route of the Strumble Shuttle, to look for wildlife of a different kind. We see seals, and a dolphin porpoising in the current, as the lighthouse flashes silently behind us. At the viewpoint, whale watchers share stories of unlikely sightings out to sea. We keep our mouths shut.

We overnight at Newgale Beach, on the route of the Puffin Shuttle, with the sliding door open to watch the surf and the walkers until we fall asleep. In the morning we wake to drizzle. Through the mist we see a horse and rider cantering across the sand. By this time we're on the route of the 411, which is disappointingly named, but still takes us to some wonderful places: Nolton Haven, Broad Haven, Druidston, St Brides, Marloes, Dale, each with its own character, and including little gems of villages, few houses, tight bends and glorious sea views. At Martin's Haven we walk out on to the cliffs

to see Skomer Island. On the beach a mother seal guards her pup, a tiny fluffy dollop resting on the sand, while Dad (we assume), a gigantic blob of a beast, elegantly cruises the bay, keeping watch. As always, we observe from a distance. We have no binoculars.

On the cliffs we look down into another bay and see dozens of seals and pups hauled out and resting while gannets, gulls and guillemots soar across the bay, far below us. Sadly, we are here too late for the puffins, which nest on Skomer in early summer.

We drive on, to Pembroke and Angle, this time following the Coastal Cruiser along the south coast to Stackpole Quay, where we load up a rucksack and stride out to find Barafundle Bay. It's long been regarded as 'one of the world's finest beaches', and is certainly one of the best in Britain because of its fine yellow sand and clear water. It feels wild, backed by dunes and with a wooded western cliff, something you don't see very often. The walk from Stackpole Quay doesn't take very long and soon we are providing the entertainment ourselves, albeit in our cossies. Thankfully the water is still warm – it's at its best in late August anyway – so we slip in without too many oohs and ahhs and swim the length of the bay and back. The cool water makes my skin tingle as I swim, and I feel more than alive. Every so often the sun, still strong, warms my back as I stroke out along the shoreline. We stop and bob, just offshore. People are watching us, perhaps intrigued that people actually swim in the sea in Wales.
They are missing out, I think.

At the end of the day we cruise into Tenby for a bag of chips and to wander around. It's bright and cheerful and people are everywhere, strolling, drinking outside pubs, playing cricket on the sand, shopping, looking out to sea. It's in great contrast to Barafundle and I love it. Floral displays fill in the gaps between the brightly painted houses and adorn lamp posts lining the maze of paths that skirt the clifftops above Castle Beach. We sit on a bench on the Esplanade and scoff our chips, looking out to sea towards Caldey Island.

We reflect on Pembrokeshire. We are at the end of a trail blazed by a fleet of tiny buses that was devised to make coastal walking a breeze. They did it and so did we, though it may have been tiny and confusing in places. We've swum in the sea, walked the coast path, found stone circles above lonely beaches, seen horses galloping across deserted sands and seen a lot of wildlife of one sort or another. And being here in Tenby, scoffing chips, sitting on a bench overlooking the sea, is a glorious, very British end to the journey. My chips – proper chip-shop chips, wrapped in paper, juicy, salty and fresh – smell and taste divine. They are.

# THE DRIVING

**WARNING 1:** At Little Haven there is a very tight bend that any vehicle over 4 metres long (13ft) will struggle with. There is an alternative route that takes less than a mile.

**WARNING 2:** There are some steep and narrow sections on this route that may challenge huge units. But big vans and smaller motorhomes will make mincemeat of it.

**CONGRATULATIONS:** One thing I really noticed when driving around Pembrokeshire was the brilliant state of the public toilets. At a time when many councils are closing them right, left and centre, Pembrokeshire's farsightedness is wonderful news for the travelling camper and a very good reason to come here above other places. Such cleanliness makes visitors feel welcomed and valued. Take note, Cornwall Council.

Ever since I first wrote about Pembrokeshire in *The Woof Guide to the Best Dog Walks in Pembrokeshire with Bob the Dog* (it's a classic, but sadly out of print) I have been a little obsessed with the Poppit Rocket and its other joyfully named counterparts. It's a bus service that runs with the sole purpose of serving the Pembrokeshire Coast Path, a designated National Trail. It connects towns with beaches and major stop-offs so that walkers can do one-way walks and then get the bus home afterwards. It's a genius idea that covers the entire coast from Cardigan to Amroth. It's also got a great name, which is part of the reason for liking it so much.

How could you not want to follow a route taken by the Poppit Rocket, the Strumble Shuttle, the Coastal Cruiser, the Celtic Coaster and the Puffin Shuttle? For me, it's a gift. The routes prove that it can be done, even though you might have to reverse a little bit sometimes. They follow little back roads, generally stay away from the main routes and take you to all the best places. You can't dawdle, especially if you get behind one of the buses themselves. I'm not going to go into too much detail here because to explain every twist and turn of the route would send you to sleep and probably into a hedge somewhere. So my advice is to look at your map (make it a good one), go online at www.pembrokeshire. gov.uk and note the routes and stops, then set off with a competent map reader by your side. The Pembrokeshire coastal lanes are narrow and often confusing, but with a steady head and a brave heart you can conquer them! And don't forget that if the Puffin Shuttle can do it, so can you.

Finally, before I give you the skinny, don't be put off if you find yourselves driving down a road with grass growing down the middle. It won't last and you won't fall into the sea. Eventually the road will get bigger, so pull in your wing mirrors and steel yourself for a brilliant ride through some lovely countryside.

The Poppit Rocket goes from Cardigan to Fishguard via Poppit Sands, Newport Sands (park on the beach for £3) and Newport. Take a detour to Bryn-henllan for a gorgeous beachside pub with good parking and a lovely beach, plus camping up the hill.

The Strumble Shuttle picks up the baton in Fishguard and takes you on a perfect seaside ramble via Strumble Head (lighthouse and whale-watching spot), Granston, Abercastle and Porthgain (stop here for sure as there are some brilliant ruins, art galleries and a great pub, plus you can plug in at a home-made aire for £15 a night). It will also take you to Abereiddy (for the Blue Lagoon) and on to St David's.

The Puffin Shuttle is the next route to follow. This will lead you on a merry dance between St David's, Solva (book early if you want a table at the lovely Cambrian Inn), Newgale (great campsite and some wild spots), Nolton Haven, Broad Haven, St Brides and Marloes. You'll then have to pick up the scent of the rather dull-sounding 315, which will take you to Dale and into Milford Haven. Between Milford

Nearest van hire

**Columbus Campervans**
● www.columbuscampervans.com

Haven and Pembroke you are on your own, but don't panic. It's easy. Follow the B4325 and the A477 to cross Milford Haven. Then, once you have negotiated Pembroke, take the B4320 to Angle and follow the route of the Coastal Cruiser. This will take you to some of the best bits of Pembrokeshire: the Green Bridge of Wales, St Govan's lovely little chapel in the rock, Bosherston Lily Ponds, Stackpole Quay (National Trust estate and tea room – great flapjack!), Barafundle Bay (the world's best, apparently) and Freshwater East.

From Freshwater East you'll need to find your way via the B4584 to the A4139. The rather dully named 348 is the route that will take you into Tenby, but don't forget about a few stops along the way, including Manorbier (beautiful village and castle with great beach) and Lydstep.

## PLACES TO STAY

Pembrokeshire has lots of campsites. It seems as if every farmer and his favourite cow now offer places to lay your hat for the night in season. This is great as it means there is a lot of choice. I could never hope to list them all here, so have included only those that I know personally and have experienced.

### West Hook Farm Camping
Marloes, Pembrokeshire, SA62 3BJ
**web:** www.westhookfarm-camping.co.uk
**email:** r.thomas122@btinternet.com
**tel:** 01646 636424

**info:** *A wild spot on a working farm near Strumble Head with sea views. Out-of-the-way perfection.*

### Newgale Campsite
Wood Hill, Newgale,
Haverfordwest, SA62 6AS
**web:** www.newgalecampsite.co.uk
**email:** enquiries@newgale
campsite.co.uk
**tel:** 07725 982550

**info:** *A very popular site right on the beach at Newgale. Best location if you like surfing or beach walking. Pub and surf shop next door.*

### Caerfai Campsite
Caerfai Farm, St David's,
Pembrokeshire, SA62 6QT
**web:** www.caerfaifarm.co.uk
**tel:** 01437 720548

**info:** *A lovely farm campsite with views overlooking the sea – and its own private beach.*

### Abereiddy
A 'wild spot' in a private car park near the Blue Lagoon. Treat with respect.

**info:** *There have been issues here, but in 2018 they have been apparently resolved with a £10 fee for overnighting and a £4 fee for day parking. Correct at the time of writing.*

### Whitesands Camping
Tan y Bryn, St David's, SA62 6PS
**web:** www.whitesandscamping.co.uk
**email:** info@whitesandscamping.co.uk
**tel:** 01437 721472

**info:** *Great location above Whitesands Beach near St David's.*

# IN THE AREA

**The Blue Lagoon** A flooded quarry at Abereiddy. Popular, but no less enticing for that. A deep-water wild swimming spot.

**TYF for Coasteering and Coastal Adventures** The guys and girls who invented the sport of coasteering. Today there might be a plethora of companies offering outdoor adventures (and why not?), but the people at TYF are the original and best in the little city with the big heart. • www.tyf.com

**St David's Cathedral** Fifteen hundred years of continual worship make this one of the holiest sites in Wales. It's lovely too.
• www.stdavids cathedral.org.uk

**Pembroke Castle** About as castle-y as a castle gets, really. A thousand years in the development

and still going strong. Plus it's the birthplace of Henry VII, Big Old Henry's dad, so it's the place where the Tudors began their exciting tour of duty as monarchs in our fair land.
• www.pembrokecastle.co.uk

**Stackpole Estate** A lovely stretch of the coast, including the quay, and an easy walk to Barafundle Bay. • www.national trust.org.uk/stackpole

**Bosherston Lily Ponds**
A beautiful walk alongside very picturesque lily ponds that lead to Broad Haven beach. Very peaceful.

**St Govan's Chapel** They say that counting the steps down to the chapel and back up again will never give you the same answer... A tiny chapel set at the bottom of a cliff reached down some steps in a ravine...
• www.visitpembrokeshire.com/ attractions-events/st-govans-chapel

# THE
# NORTH WEST

The Lake District is a great place to drive, as
long as you do it at the right time of the year. I drove its
passes and along its lakes in the deep midwinter. The roads
were clear, the villages deserted and the peaks covered in snow.
It may have been cold but there was always a warm welcome on
the open-all-year campsites and in the cosy pubs. During the day
I climbed snowy peaks and even swam in cold, clear water.
You can too, with the right day, a deep breath and a good
map. Don't wait for the weather. It's grim up north,
and that's the way we like it.

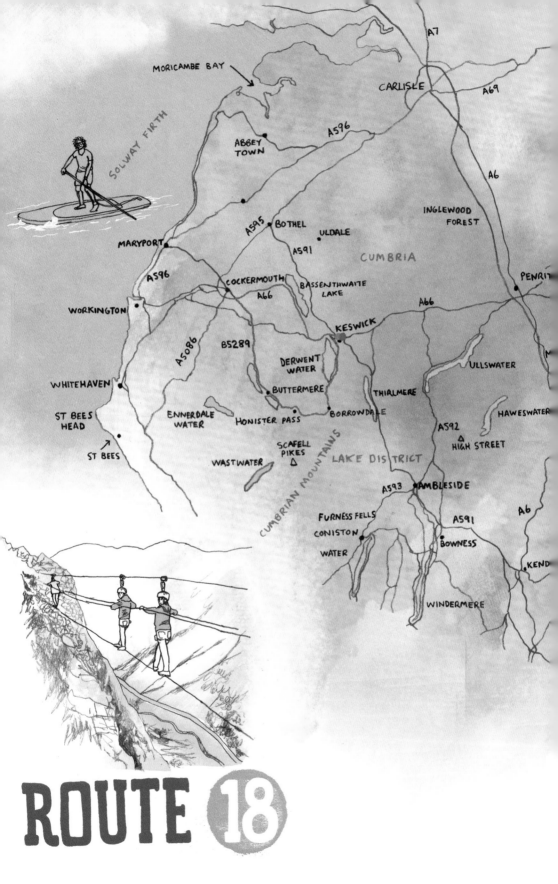

MORICAMBE BAY

A7

CARLISLE

A69

SOLWAY FIRTH

ABBEY TOWN

A596

A6

INGLEWOOD FOREST

MARYPORT

A595  BOTHEL

ULDALE

CUMBRIA

PENRITH

A596

A591

COCKERMOUTH

A66

BASSENTHWAITE LAKE

A66

WORKINGTON

KESWICK

ULLSWATER

A5086

B5289

DERWENT WATER

THIRLMERE

HAWESWATER

WHITEHAVEN

ENNERDALE WATER

BUTTERMERE

BORROWDALE

A592

HIGH STREET

ST BEES HEAD

HONISTER PASS

SCAFELL PIKES △

CUMBRIAN MOUNTAINS

LAKE DISTRICT

ST BEES

WASTWATER

A593  AMBLESIDE

A6

FURNESS FELLS

A591

CONISTON WATER

BOWNESS

KENDAL

WINDERMERE

# ROUTE ⑱

# KESWICK AND BORROWDALE

## WANDERINGS IN MIDDLE EARTH

Borrowdale sounds like it belongs in Middle Earth, or some other kingdom of the gods. And so it should. It's my idea of a perfect English dale, an Elysian flat-bottomed valley surrounded by white-capped peaks. Getting there is easy – unless the road from Keswick is closed, in which case you'll have to take a detour via Lorton Fells. But that's no biggie, if you discount Honister Pass.

BEST FOR:
**Lakeside picnics and paddles**

START/END:
**Keswick**

MILEAGE: **34 miles (55 kilometres)**

DAYS TO EXPLORE: **1**

OS LANDRANGER MAP: **89**

THE NORTH WEST

241

**We drive out of Keswick on the B2589.** We are on our way to Buttermere to unfurl our blow-up paddleboards (SUPs) and explore the lake. We hear that it's the clearest of them all, and that's enough for us. We set our course for Borrowdale and drive.

Only there's a problem. The road is closed. We don't know how far up it's closed or whether there is any access to the other side. From the map we see that the road is the only way to access Buttermere from this side. We make the decision to take the long way round and approach Lorton Vale from the west. We take the A66 out of Keswick and find our way to the unnamed road that meets up with the B5292 to take us through Low Lorton and on to Crummock Water.

There are 'road closed' signs here too, saying there is no access to Keswick from this side. We ignore them and continue past Crummock Water and on to Buttermere. We drive through the village and find a parking spot at the side of the lake on its eastern shore. There are a few people walking and some picnicking on the lakeside, and a gentle breeze is ruffling the surface of the water. The sun is bright and cool, backlighting the trees and leaving the western shore in shadow. Red Pike (755m/2,477ft), High Stile (806m/2,644ft) and High Crag (744m/2,440ft) are covered with a dusting of snow that fills the crags and crevices but leaves the dark outcrops of rock looking black in contrast. The lake, as predicted, is clear.

I pull on my wetsuit and prepare the SUPs for a paddle. When I wade into the water I feel an instant hit of cold water, even through 5mm of expensive neoprene. The water is very cold, at about four or five degrees centigrade. I make a mental note not to fall in. The visibility in the water is really incredible, and we can see the bottom until we get out into the middle of the lake where it's around 24m (78ft) deep.

We paddle our way back to the lakeshore and roll up the SUPs. Once we've put them away I suggest to Liz that we have a skinny-dip. Or at least swim once we've got our wetsuits off. She thinks it's a mad idea but why not? We have swum in the sea every month so far: in December we took part in a Christmas Day swim and in November we swam from a quiet cove on the north coast of Cornwall. How bad is four degrees anyway?

It's cold. I run into the water wearing nothing but my shorts and a pair of wetsuit boots. It's not a glamorous look in any way, but who cares? We are the only ones here. I wade in quickly, huffing and puffing as I sink into the water, and take a few strokes before clambering out on to the bank again. My skin tingles with the cold and my heart is racing but I feel alive, that's for sure. Next it's Liz's turn. She wades in quickly and dunks, blowing out constantly to avoid cold-water shock.

We dress quickly and press on, up and over Honister Pass towards Keswick. We have no idea if the road is open, but we want to explore Borrowdale before it gets too late. The drive up Honister is astounding, one of those glorious roads that feels like a challenge but is also astoundingly beautiful. It snakes up the narrow rocky valley, almost immediately above the treeline, and rising to 355m (1,164ft). We stop at the top, on the road adjacent to the slate mine (open since 1643), to admire the views. But we decide we must press on. The afternoon is getting on and the temperature is dropping fast: we don't want to be up here when it gets dark, as the road is steep and slippery enough as it is.

We descend into Borrowdale and I am absolutely flabbergasted by how it looks. There are mature oaks and copses of firs dotted between green fields bordered by stone walls. It's an open landscape, almost too good to be true, a paradise of Elysian fields, the River Derwent running through it to Derwentwater and Keswick. But then Borrowdale has been in the capable hands of the National Trust for generations, so it stands to reason it should be like this. The dale has been admired and used in literature by John Ruskin, Beatrix Potter and Alfred Wainwright.

We wonder if we are going to have to stay here the night. I wouldn't mind at all, and we note Chapel House Farm as we trundle by, in case we need to turn around and bed down there rather than going back over Honister Pass. A few miles later we come across a road gang. We stop, wondering if they'll flag us down and turn us back. But they are removing their signs and opening the road. We are the first to go through, and cruise easily down the deserted road, past Derwentwater and straight into Keswick.

# THE DRIVING

If you've got a head for passes you can see Borrowdale in a couple of ways that make up a loop. It's possible to go up the Newlands Pass, which has some steep sections, or up the Whinlatter Pass, which is one of the easiest of the Lakes passes. Or you can do what we did, which is to take the A66 out of Keswick along Bassenthwaite Lake. It's a fast road, but you don't have to do it quickly, and the first part of it is really nice. But it's not until you turn off around Lambfoot for Lorton, on an unnamed road heading towards the B5292, that it starts to get good. The B5292 heads north over Whinlatter Pass, so you'll need to veer right on to the B5289 at Lorton to get to Crummock Water and Buttermere. It's a lovely drive along a single-track road with passing places, with a few places to stop right by the lakeside. Follow this road to Buttermere. There are parking places at either end of the lake. From Buttermere the road segues nicely into Honister Pass, a great snaking, twisting road that goes steeply up to the pass over the course of a couple of miles. At the top the views are spectacular. From there it's a steep descent to Borrowdale and Derwentwater. You can't get lost.

## PLACES TO STAY

**Chapel House Farm Campsite**
Chapel House Farm, Borrowdale, Cumbria, CA12 5XG
**web:** www.chapelhousefarmcampsite.co.uk
**email:** info@chapelhousefarmcampsite.co.uk
**tel:** 01768 777256

**info:** *A small site in the heart of Borrowdale. Amazing base for walking.*

**Keswick Camping and Caravanning Site**
Crow Park Road, Keswick, Cumbria, CA12 5EP
**web:** www.campingandcaravanningclub.co.uk
**tel:** 01768 772392

**info:** *Nice friendly site on the banks of the Derwent. Open all year, so perfect for winter wanderings.*

## IN THE AREA

**Via Ferrata**  A via ferrata is a mountain route made up of ladders, ropes and steps banged into sheer cliff faces. This one, at the top of Honister Pass, is allegedly the best one in England and will take you up the original path miners at the slate mines took. There is also an extreme version, which, frankly, you can keep.  • **www.honister.com**

**The Bowder Stone**  An improbably landed rock that balances on one edge in the middle of Borrowdale. Park at Bowder Stone Car Park near Grange and walk 15 minutes. There's a ladder to the top. A bit mad.  • **www.visitcumbria.com/kes/the-bowder-stone**

**Whinlatter Forest & Visitor Centre**
At the top of Whinlatter Pass, an award-winning Forestry Commission centre with walking trails, mountain bike trails and a Go Ape course.  • **www.forestry.gov.uk/whinlatter**

Nearest van hire

**Rainbow Campers**
• www.vwcamperhire.net

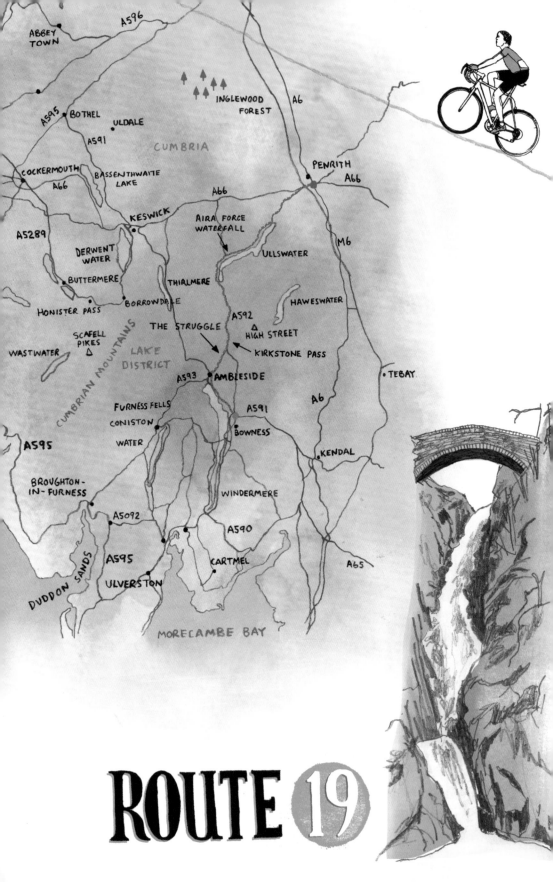

ROUTE 19

# KIRKSTONE PASS

## YOU TAKE THE HIGH ROAD

The road from Windermere to Penrith via Ullswater and the Kirkstone Pass is a cracker, especially in winter. It's the Lake District's highest road, at 454m (1,489ft) above sea level. As such, it's the one they close first, so you've probably heard it mentioned on the travel news more than a few times.

BEST FOR:
**Views, walking, snow in winter**

START:
**Windermere**

END: **Penrith**

MILEAGE: **24 miles (39 kilometres)**

DAYS TO EXPLORE: **1**

OS LANDRANGER MAP: **90**

THE NORTH WEST

**The pass is closed.** Or so they said yesterday, and unlikely to open anytime soon. It's impassable, dangerous for cars, drive with care.

Normally that kind of news would put me off. But this is the last day of our slow road tour of the Lakes and it's the one route that's missing: the one I wanted to try. We've been warned against taking the route up to Kirkstone Pass that's called 'The Struggle', and I don't want to find out why. It's a steep, short climb of 20% from Ambleside. Instead we take the A592 from Windermere, the longer and less steep of the two routes up to the pass. It's not a dawdler, though. As soon as we're out of Windermere we're climbing, through the trees at first, winding around lazy bends past cottages and lovely big trees. Once we reach Town Head we come out of the trees and into more open country. The wooded valley at Troutbeck lies to our right as we continue to climb, heading westwards over the top of the valley. Ahead lie the peaks of Troutbeck Tongue, Ill Bell and Kentmere Pike, snow covered.

We round a bend and suddenly we get a sense of scale. We can see down into the dale that carries Stock Ghyll, the stream that runs through Ambleside. Beyond that lies the head of Windermere, glinting in the sun.

Surprisingly, the road is clear and we make easy progress up to the parking area at the head of the pass. We are not alone. The car park is busy and we are lucky to get a space for ourselves. A cold wind is blowing but it doesn't stop people from tiptoeing across the ice-covered car park to the muddy gate, stepping over the peaty, wet ground on a few tiny stepping stones. I worry sometimes about these people who are wearing trainers without socks on a very cold day. Some have no coats, while Liz and I are dressed in our long johns, overtrousers, skiing jackets, hats and gloves. Perhaps living in Cornwall has made us nesh?

We have no sledge so we decide to hike up to St Raven's Edge, the highest point on the east side of the pass. The snow is deep and the path is steep and difficult to find. We walk in a series of hairpins to mitigate the climb, following in the deep footsteps of others who have been up here before us.

At the top there is a cairn where the wind has sculpted the snow into strange shapes. We stand on it, the highest point on our trip here, and look down towards Ullswater and Brothers Water. We can see our route ahead of us, stretching away into the distance. Once we descend we will pass by Brothers Water and then skirt the village of Patterdale before following the north bank of Ullswater. Soon after we know we'll be back on one of the green roads on our map, the A66, and then soon after that the M6, which will take us south towards home.

I look around and feel a longing to be here longer. The Lake District has completely blown me away with its beauty, its accessibility, the scale of the landscape and the size of the trees. It seems they live longer around here.

Last time I was here it rained incessantly. This time we haven't had a drop.

I vow to return in the summer.

# THE DRIVING

The A592 takes a direct course up Kirkstone Pass from Windermere all the way to the edge of the National Park at the junction with the A66 near Penrith. It's a classic Lakes drive on a good road that's popular for its own sake, particularly among motorcyclists. There is a bit of a challenge to it too, although I don't think I'd recommend doing The Struggle. The drive

## PLACES TO STAY

**Gillside Farm**
Glenridding by Ullswater, Cumbria, CA11 0QQ
**web:** www.gillsidecaravanandcampingsite.co.uk
**tel:** 01768 482346

**info:** *Campsite on a working farm at the foot of Helvellyn on Ullswater. Perfectly placed for Kirkstone Pass.*

out of Windermere is a delight, revealing new sights around each corner, particularly when you round the bend at Troutbeck Tongue to see the top of Lake Windermere for the first time. That's a beauty. From there it's a short roll (almost) into the pass.

Dropping down to Brothers Water is an equally lovely roll. The road twists in easy, slow curves as it drops down the side of the U-shaped valley into the floor. It's a classic glacial landscape with steep-sided peaks rising up sharply from the valley floor.

Beyond Patterdale you'll find Glenridding, a lakeside stop with shop, hotel and coffee shop on the lakeshore of Ullswater. It's a lovely spot that leads you along the north shore of the lake, offering fantastic views of the way you just came. A stop at the jetty at Aira Force waterfall gives you a great chance to stop and look back. We did. Between the peaks we saw Kirkstone Pass in the sunshine, with the peaks themselves coloured perfectly in receding hues.

# IN THE AREA

**Walking**  It's the Lake District! What else are you going to do?

**Aira Force Waterfall**  An absolutely stunning circular walk to and from this lovely waterfall that's National Trust owned. There is a fine collection of trees here too, all named and marked.
● www.nationaltrust.org.uk/aira-force-and-ullswater

**Treetop Trek**  A treetop adventure for kids of five and upwards. Off the A591, Brockhole.  ● **www.treetoptrek.co.uk**

Nearest van hire

**Rainbow Camper Hire**
● www.vwcamperhire.net

CUMBRIA

WORKINGTON

A66 PENRITH

KESWICK

WHITEHAVEN

ULLSWATER

BUTTERMERE

THIALMERE

ST BEES
HEAD

ENNERDALE
WATER

HONISTER PASS

BORROWDALE

HAWESWAT

A592

ST BEES

SCAFELL
PIKES △

CUMBRIAN MOUNTAINS

HIGH STREET

WASTWATER

LAKE
DISTRICT

A593 AMBLESIDE

A595

FURNESS FELLS

A6

A591

OLD MAN
OF CONISTON →

CONISTON

BOWNESS

GRIZEDALE
FOREST →

KEN

BEATRIX POTTER

BROUGHTON-
IN-FURNESS

WINDERMERE

A5092

A590

CARTMEL

A595

DUDDON SANDS

ULVERSTON

MORECAMBE BAY

# ROUTE 20

# WINDERMERE AND CONISTON

## THE BACK OF BEYOND

The Lake District has long been popular. It's been muse, folly and friend to many a literary genius, from Beatrix Potter and Arthur Ransome to Samuel Taylor Coleridge, John Ruskin and William Wordsworth. That it's been a hotbed of creative writing and thinking for a long time is reflected in the landscape: as a protected area, it has big trees, well-managed footpaths and a lot of great roads. And this particular one could well be the slowest of them all.

BEST FOR:
**Taking your time, lakes and views**

START:
Coniston

END: Coniston

MILEAGE: **39 miles (62 kilometres)**

DAYS TO EXPLORE: **2**

OS LANDRANGER MAP: **97 (90)**

**We're here out of season,** thank goodness, otherwise we're not sure we'd ever have made it down this road. Like all the roads in the Lake District National Park we've driven over the last few days, it's small, winding and barely wide enough for two cars to pass. So whether it turns out to have been for the best or not, we have taken about the smallest of all the small roads we could have taken and are rattling down the eastern shore of Coniston Water.

We travel between the meadows and the woods, looking down at the water across gently sloping meadows, where dots of white sheep graze peacefully in the quiet. There is snow on the Old Man of Coniston on the opposite bank, making the whole scene look terribly bucolic. The sky is a weak blue, the fields are green despite the time of the year, and the woods, despite the lack of leaves on a lot of the beeches and oaks, are dense and dark. A small moss-covered stone wall separates us from the meadows.

The road is slow. It meanders gently around cottages, grand homes set in wooded glades, tea rooms and the occasional muddy car park. Further on we come to a section that's almost on the water, where the stone wall gives way to a post-and-rail fence. There are stopping points on the bank where you'd love to linger, casting your line, launching your dinghy or just taking an hour for a rest. For this reason it's perfect and has all the elements I've been looking for: water, trees and fields, with mountains and vistas beyond. It's a leafy lane like you'll find all over

England if you know where to look. It could be the Chilterns, or Cornwall or the Peaks, except it's not, because brooding, white capped and heavy on the opposite bank is the Old Man of Coniston, the mountain that surveys it all.

It's no wonder Ruskin, who bought Brantwood in 1871, looked over the view of Coniston and declared it to be the 'best in all of England'.

We continue south to the bottom end of Coniston Water and head up the west side of Windermere on another road that's tiny, seeking a route through to Hawkshead via the Windermere Ferry. This time it's less obvious which way to go and we meander and dip our way along the lakeside, sometimes high in the hills, sometimes down deep dips, and at other times lost in the orange carpet of dropped beech leaves. It's lovely exploring. We come out at Far Sawrey, the tiny port where we take the shortcut to Windermere. We carry on around the lake and find a beautiful wide-open area on the banks where there are a few places to stop. We dutifully apply the brakes and set up for lunch on the waterside.

It turns out this is a dead end to us. Entry to the west shore is restricted beyond this point, so we head up the B5285 towards Hawkshead, making a detour to Grizedale Forest and then to Tarn Hows, one of the most visited spots in Lakeland. It was once owned by Beatrix Potter, who bequeathed it to the National Trust. On summer days it's jam-packed with people, but on this day it's empty save for a few cars in the car park, that we presume belong to the wardens. We stop and look over the tarn as the sun and temperature drop. It's so peaceful and quiet and it's hard to imagine it any other way. But the one-way system tells us otherwise. It's a honeypot and we can see why. And we're lucky to see it on such a cool, clear, lovely day in winter.

# THE DRIVING

Have I already hinted that the Lake District might be tricky in high season for a big vehicle? Well, if you haven't got it yet, please take it from me that unless you can reverse your unit – a lot – and don't mind steep hills and narrow spaces, you'd do best to leave it until everyone else has gone home.

That's the warning done with, now let's get on with the drive ... this is magical. Set out from Coniston on the B5285 towards Hawkshead. You'll

skirt the northern end of the lake. Take a right signposted to Monk Coniston down the single-track road that follows the eastern shore. It's a narrow meandering kind of a single-track road with a few passing spaces but not a lot. This is where you'll have to do some reversing. It's also a bit on the narrow side, so if you're more than 6' 6" wide or in a 40ft Winnebago you might want to give it a miss.

It's a beautiful drive down to the southern end of Coniston Water and you'll skirt the shore most of the way. There are some car parks dotted along the length of the road where you can stop to put the kettle on. The lake is five miles long and the fifth largest of the lakes. It was the place Sir Malcolm Campbell chose to set his world water speed record in 1939 and the place where his son, Donald Campbell, lost his life breaking the 300mph mark in 1967.

At the southern end of Coniston the road meets the A5084, where you take a left, then, soon after, another left on to the A5092. This busy road will take you to a roundabout with the junction of the A590. This will take you to Newby Bridge, where you'll need to take another left over the River Leven and then follow the road around to the left, following the signs for 'Lakeside Steamers'. This will take you up into the hills on the west shore of Windermere. It's a good road that passes through a mixture of open country and wooded hillside. At Graythwaite Estate there is an option to take a right to the ferry, but it's another narrow road and not recommended. Instead, carry on to Esthwaite Water and take a right to Near Sawrey. At Near Sawrey you'll hit the B5285, which will take you down to the ferry. Just before the ferry there is a left turn which will take you along the shore opposite Belle Isle – park here for great lake views or turn around and head back up the B5285 for Hawkshead village.

After Hawkshead you can take the one-way loop up to Tarn Hows by taking a right turn just after Hawkshead Hill. This is a magnificent road that climbs steadily upwards through forests of pine and birch and bracken, with stone walls either side. When it eventually comes out at Tarn Hows you'll get another of the Lake District's best views: it's all spread out before you. There is a car park, together with plenty of accessible paths around the tarn. The road down is steep and tricky, but at least you can guarantee there will be nothing coming the other way – it's one way! Once back at the B5285 you're almost back at Coniston. Job done. Time for a pint.

# IN THE AREA

**Grizedale Forest** There's a great bunch of stuff here, from mountain bike trails and walking trails to a nice café and exhibition space. Kids will love the sculpture trail, complete with musical trees...
- www.forestry.gov.uk/grizedale

### Wordsworth's Hawkshead
Wordsworth attended Hawkshead Grammar School. You can visit it and see the desk wot the poet laureate scratched his name on . . .
- www.hawksheadgrammar.org.uk

### In Search of Peter
**Rabbit** Beatrix Potter was one of Hawkshead's more famous residents. You can see some of her original artwork at the Beatrix Potter Gallery and see her house at Hill Top. Both are owned by the National Trust.
- www.nationaltrust.org.uk/hill-top

### Nearest van hire
**Lakes Camper Hire**
- www.lakescamperhire.co.uk

# PLACES TO STAY

**Coniston Park Coppice Site**
Park Gate, Coniston, Cumbria, LA21 8LA
**web:** www.caravanclub.co.uk
**tel:** 01539 441555

**info:** *A big site with plenty of hardstanding among the trees, great facilities and lakeside access for small craft and rubber duckies.*

**THE NORTH**

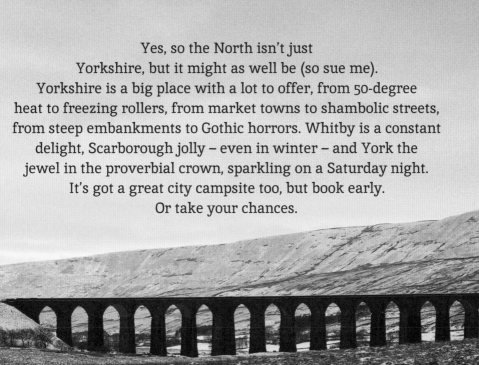

Yes, so the North isn't just
Yorkshire, but it might as well be (so sue me).
Yorkshire is a big place with a lot to offer, from 50-degree
heat to freezing rollers, from market towns to shambolic streets,
from steep embankments to Gothic horrors. Whitby is a constant
delight, Scarborough jolly – even in winter – and York the
jewel in the proverbial crown, sparkling on a Saturday night.
It's got a great city campsite too, but book early.
Or take your chances.

ROUTE **21**

# HARROGATE AND WHARFEDALE

## WHEN IN ROME

Harrogate sits at the southern and eastern end of the Dales and on the A59, the route that crosses the National Park. Heading north from the A59, there are some of the loveliest dales and becks, and even a couple of well-known waterfalls. We explored Wharfedale and Littondale. But not before freshening up at Harrogate's famous Turkish Baths.

BEST FOR:
**Hotting up**

START:
**Harrogate**

END: **Bolton Abbey**

MILEAGE: **78 miles (125 kilometres)**

DAYS TO EXPLORE: **2**

OS LANDRANGER MAP: **104, 99, 98**

We walk into reception. It is light and airy and painted bright white, with comfy-looking sofas and glass tables scattered with brochures and magazines. We walk up to the reception desk and say hello to the receptionist, unsure of what to ask for or how to approach the subject.

'Er. We've come to see if we can have a Turkish bath,' I say.
'Yes, of course,' replies the receptionist. 'Now?'
'Yes, if that's possible.'
'Yes. We have a mixed session starting in ten minutes.'
'OK. Thanks. What's a mixed session?'
'You've not been here before, have you?'
'No.'
'OK, well it's very simple...'

And with that we are ushered through reception and into a corridor of dark wood panelling with a coloured, tiled floor. It's as if we are stepping from the modern world into a Victorian sanatorium. The building is beautiful – it was and still is the flagship of Harrogate's 'spa experience' – with polished brass, deeply waxed wood and original features everywhere. It feels very grand and dignified.

The smiling staff wear crisp white uniforms, the women with buns pulled back hard, away from their faces. They give us towels and lead us to an area of changing rooms with heavy curtains. I ask if I can take pictures, but no, it's not allowed. It's understandable, of course, because, beyond the chenille, I can see men and women lying on dark-coloured wooden loungers, wearing fluffy bathrobes, bikinis and shorts. So instead of snapping the lovely surroundings – I can see a glimpse of the Moorish-looking interior amid the fluffy robes – I pretend I am on some kind of undercover assignment. This involves taking out my GoPro and filming a little to-camera piece of video in the changing room. I whisper, trying not to alert the staff, feeling a bit stupid, and deciding very quickly to avoid any kind of scene and just enjoy the experience instead of papping it and getting into trouble.

I have never been to a Turkish bath before and I have no idea how to bathe in a Turkish style, so I try to remain open and willing to go along with anything, even though I am a bit nervous. The hot room, so I hear, is 70 degrees centigrade, which makes me wonder how I am going to breathe, or even survive. I change into my shorts and wander out into the 'cool room',

which, at 35 degrees, is really not that cold at all. We sit and Lizzy asks me if I'd like a massage. She goes off and books one for me in an hour's time, for half an hour, while I sweat a little. When she comes back we get ready to head into the baths proper. We walk past the plunge pool, which, at 20 degrees, is warmer than the sea by a long way. We make our way into the first of the bath's hot rooms. It's warm, at 45 degrees centigrade, a heat that is supposed to get you used to the heat. I'm OK with it and sit for a few minutes, tiny beads of sweat forming on my forehead. I look around. The

tiled ceiling is vaulted and there are Moroccan arches between the rooms, which lead away from me. The room I am in is about 4.5m (15ft) square and has a series of tiled concrete plinths around the outside, with wooden chairs draped with towels, and, in some cases, hot-looking people. I look at the mosaic floor. With the exception of a motif border running around the outside, it's like a crazy paving of white, black, yellow, red and brown pieces, the water on the floor making some of them shine like jewels.

I'm not good with temperatures above 30, but this is OK, I think. I joke that I am 'temperate man', a special, slightly fragile kind of human that cannot survive outside the temperate zones, but I am still OK when I enter the warm room. That one's set at 55 degrees, which is a nice day in the desert. Surprisingly, it's not stifling or claustrophobic and, miracle of miracles, I am able to breathe, although my sweat glands are working overtime. Droplets are running down my back, into my eyes and down between my buttocks.

After a few minutes I have to cool off, so I head for the shower room and rinse off with a warm shower. It's refreshing. Then it's off to the hottest

room. We've been warned not to spend too long in there, so I am ready to make a dash for it. We place our towels on one of the three long wooden benches and sit down. They are arse-burningly hot and I can manage only a few minutes, fully recumbent. I heat up, knowing that in a few minutes I will be heading for the tepid – but no doubt refreshing – waters of the plunge pool.

Compared with the 70 degrees I have just come out of, 20 is very cold indeed. I'm not usually one of those ooch, ouch, eek dippers who take ages to inch into the sea,

but I can't hurry this immersion. Liz half dives and half pushes off into a quick breaststroke. I follow, keeping my head above water and pushing out breaths like someone in labour to avoid ingesting gulps of pool water. It's invigorating, and I soon get used to the tingling of my skin.

I think, when I shower off after my massage in a warm, blue-tiled shower room, that this is an infinitely better experience than dashing across a snowy campsite to stand under a dribble of warm water in a cubicle in a toilet block. It feels like an expensive indulgence, a luxury. But it's just the tonic we need on a cold day in February when the temperature is little above freezing and sleet is drifting down outside.

When we leave the sanctuary of the bathhouse it starts to snow again, so we gather our coats to our chins and head for the nearest coffee shop. Sometimes you have to take it slow.

# HEXHAM TO BARNARD CASTLE

## MIDDLE ENGLAND CROSSING

A route through the North Pennines that goes slap bang through the middle of England, crossing three counties in the process. It's wild, beautiful, and has some high spots, tumbling falls and impressive castle ruins.

BEST FOR: **Big vistas and open country**

START: **Hexham**

END: **Barnard Castle**

MILEAGE: **52 miles (83 kilometres)**

DAYS TO EXPLORE: **2**

OS LANDRANGER MAP: **86, 91**

Climbing out of Haydon Bridge, I'm really not sure that we're doing the right thing. We have no idea what lies ahead of us as we trundle up the A686 towards Langley. Whatever it is, it's likely to be white, fluffy and cold, seeing as snow is almost all we've had on this trip. It's a great road and we are enjoying the climb, away from the lowlands that separate the Northumberland National Park from the North Pennines. At Langley we cross over into an Area of Outstanding Natural Beauty and come out of the trees and into open farming country. It's a whiteout, and it's only when we arrive at the hairpin bend above Cupola Bridge that we can see, for the first time, what we're in for. But the road is clear, and so far it's been great driving.

As we cross Ouston Fell I am starting to get very fractious. The snow is beginning to settle on the road and we have no idea how high we're going to have to go before we reach the zenith. We drop into Alston and find the B6277, which, we hope, will take us safely to the Tees Valley and Darlington, where a cup of tea at Nick's house awaits.

We climb quickly, reaching open moorland in moments. Up here the road has been gritted, but the fresh snowfall is covering it up quickly. We follow the tracks of cars that have been up here before us, occasionally losing our grip through the deeper drifts. In the valley to our right is the South Tyne and, soon after, at Harwood, the watershed for both the Tyne and Harwood Beck that joins the Tees a few miles down the road.

A car has stopped by the side of the road, its wheels deep in a drift. We stop to ask if they are OK. They say yes, they are about to go snowboarding. We ask about the road ahead. It's OK, they reassure us. No problem. Relieved, we carry on and stop at Harwood for a play in the snow. Lizzy has been dying to get out of the van for the last few miles, itching to make the most of the weather. Now we know it's going to get better I feel OK to stop. We stop at Harwood and climb over a stone wall into a field where there is a deep drift. In the next field there is a flock of sheep, clambering through drifts to find out what the excitement is about. They press themselves against the gate to get a better view of us throwing snowballs and sinking into the drifts, sinking into the drifts themselves.

We leave them with a snow shepherd that we built to watch over them, and carry on down Teesdale for our well-earned cup of tea.

KIELDER FOREST

NORTHUMBERLAND

WARK FOREST

A1

A6079

A696

STEEL RIGG

B6318

HADRIAN'S WALL

NEWCASTLE UPON TYNE

GREENHEAD

HAYDON BRIDGE

A69

BRAMPTON

A69

A69

HEXHAM

A695

A1

LAMBLEY

WHITFIELD

CUPOLA BRIDGE

A68

A686

A692

A693

CONSETT

ALSTON

B6295

DURHAM

A691

GARRIGILL

COWSHILL

A68

DURHAM

A689

A167

A686

PENRITH

ROUTE 23

# GATESHEAD TO GREENHEAD VIA HADRIAN'S WALL

## THE LONG, STRAIGHT ROAD

This route will take you from the heart of Newcastle, out of the city and along parts of the Roman road that follow the course of Hadrian's Wall. From the Baltic Centre for Contemporary Art it's 40 miles, almost in a straight line, to Greenhead through some of England's wildest countryside. Stop, look at the wall and enjoy visions of the life of a Roman sentry sent to this outpost at the northern edge of the Empire. Brrrr.

BEST FOR:
**Walls, Roman buildings, wild country**

START:
**Gateshead**

END: **Greenhead**

MILEAGE:
**38 miles (61 kilometres)**

DAYS TO EXPLORE: **2**

OS LANDRANGER MAP: **86, 87, 88**

THE NORTH

289

**John pulls up behind us in the lay-by.** We've stopped on a long, straight section of the Roman road between Newcastle and Carlisle and the wind is blowing hard. Patches of weak winter sunshine do their best to penetrate the gloomy white clouds that move fast across the vast and empty sky. The road disappears ahead of us into its vanishing point, the brow of a hill in an ancient and brutal landscape. It's wild up here in the old hinterland between the Roman Empire and those wild, uncontrollable Picts.

The wind rocks the van and almost pulls the door out of my hands as I open it. I step out and John is there, at the leeward side of the van, with hand outstretched. He starts the conversation by asking me what it's like to drive. It's OK, actually, I reply. It's a Benimar, based on a Fiat Ducato, a standard chassis for a coachbuilt.

He tells me he's looking for a motorhome so that he can go exploring. He had a caravan, but now he's on his own it's too much trouble, too difficult. He doesn't want to sit at home and rot. He wants to get out there and see the world. We start to talk and I realise this man is fascinating, but lonely. He needs company and time, so we give it to him. He tells us he stopped here because it's a place he used to stop with his children and grandchildren. He would come up here from his home in Newcastle, with his wife too, and

# IN THE AREA

**The Sill** The UK's National Landscape Discovery Centre can be found at Once Brewed on the B6318. It's a magnificent green building that's built from 80% local materials by local labour. It houses a café, a shop, lecture theatres and meeting spaces as well as YHA accommodation and designated motorhome parking (although no overnighting at present).
• www.thesill.org.uk

**Crag Lough and Steel Rigg** One of the best places to see Hadrian's Wall. A small car park on the north side of the B6318 opposite The Sill will take you right there. Great views. • www.northumberlandnationalpark.org.uk/places-to-visit/hadrians-wall/steel-rigg

**Open-air Pool at Haltwhistle** From April to September you can swim at Haltwhistle open-air pool. Don't panic – it's heated!
• www.haltwhistleleisure.co.uk

**Hexham** A lovely Tyneside town that's plump with history and has lots of surviving 'oldest stuff', including Hexham Abbey (AD678), the oldest purpose-built prison in England and one of the world's oldest railway stations. Plus, you can buy LPG from Hexham Garden Machinery.
• www.visithexham.net

The far North East of England
is this country's best-kept secret. It's quiet
and cool, vast and empty, with huge forests and
long walls, beautiful castles and amazing beaches. Come
here to cycle, walk, swim, surf and explore, and drive away
happy knowing you beat the crowds. Hadrian's Wall is one of
my favourite drives in the whole country, simply because the
road is straight and the wall is there. The mere fact that it
exists is astounding. Go and see it. To the east, the coast of
Northumberland sits silently waiting for you to find it.
Not many do, and that's why it is excellent
– among the best.

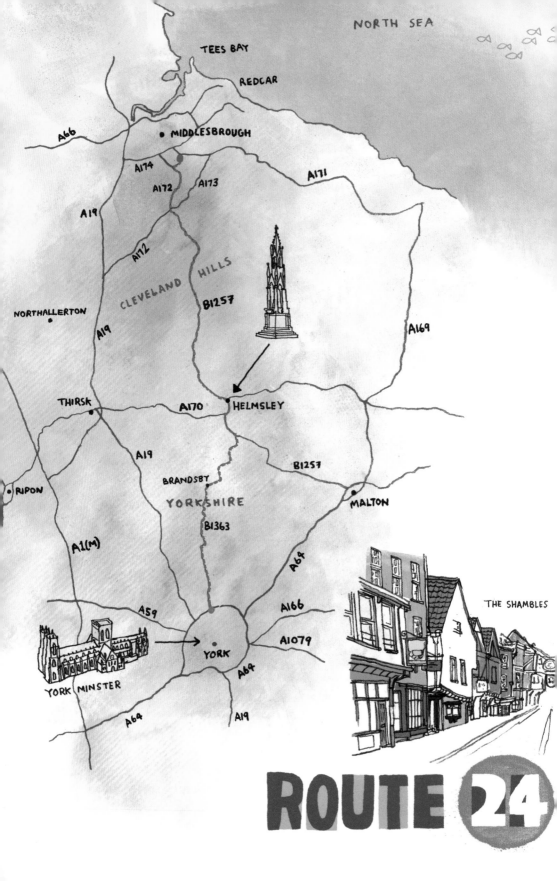

NORTH SEA

TEES BAY

REDCAR

MIDDLESBROUGH

A66

A174

A172 A173 A171

A19

A172

CLEVELAND HILLS

B1257

A169

NORTHALLERTON

A19

THIRSK

A170 HELMSLEY

A19

BRANDSBY

B1257

RIPON

YORKSHIRE

MALTON

B1363

A1(M)

A64

A59

A166

A1079

YORK

A64

A64

A19

YORK MINSTER

THE SHAMBLES

ROUTE 24

# YORK AND NORTH YORKSHIRE

## CITY CAMPING AND PEOPLE WATCHING

York is more than just a stop-off on the map. It's a brilliant place to camp – as long as you book early – and a wonderful city to explore using the campsite as your base. Heading as far north as York gives you plenty of opportunity to test the brakes, wind your way up stunning hills and see some of England's loveliest medieval architecture before you crack on even further north.

BEST FOR:
**City camping/ pootling north**

START: **York**

END: **Teesside**

MILEAGE: **50 miles (80 kilometres)**

DAYS TO EXPLORE: **2**

OS LANDRANGER MAP: **93, 100, 105**

**It's Saturday and we are lucky (again).** We called ahead to book the Caravan and Motorhome Club Site in York, at Rowntree Park (yes, it is named after the sweets empire) and managed to secure a pitch – the last pitch – on this popular open-all-year site. It is the busiest site on the network and pitches – even in the depths of winter – are like gold dust. So yes, we are very lucky indeed. After spending time in the Peaks we need a wash and brush-up and the chance to empty our tanks and spruce ourselves and our onboard tanks up before hitting the road north out of the city.

But first we have to get there. Take a look at the club's directory and you'll see that there is an approved way of arriving at the site, via a small road that runs between the end of a series of terraced streets, past the Slip Inn and on to Terry Avenue, the small road that follows the south bank of the River Ouse and that takes you as far as the very popular Rowntree Park.

The site is perfectly situated for a city stay as it's just a five-minute walk from the city centre.

The only thing that's stopping us from getting there is Skeldergate Bridge, which goes over Terry Avenue. It's low. I don't think we'll get under it, so I stop and get out. It's close, but the Benimar is about six inches (15cm) too tall. We back up. The road is narrow and there's nowhere to perform a three-point turn, so we must back out on to Skeldergate. It's not such a drama for us as we're in a motorhome, but we wonder how many caravanners have been caught out down here without reading the directory. More fool us. Even more fool them.

We pitch up and get ready for a night out in York. It's a rare treat for us to go wandering in the evening as we usually cook, open a beer or two and then crash. Even if we stay on a Britstop we often make it only as far as the bar, so this chance to crawl a bit, eat a bit and see a bit has to be relished. We step out of the van into a dry, moonlit night and crunch out of the site on the gravel, peeking into some of the other motorhomes and caravans as we go. We see couples and families sitting down to watch huge flat screen TVs. We haven't watched a telly for

almost three weeks now, so it's disappointing to see others squandering this precious time. Even on snowed-in evenings and rainy nights Liz and I manage to avoid watching screens when we're away from home. It's part of what makes going away so good. It's the time away from all the vapid trappings of everyday existence that makes it special for us. Life lived away from the sofa.

We turn into The Shambles, a street that's famous for its overhanging timber-framed medieval buildings. The name, apparently, comes from *Fleshammels*, the Anglo-Saxon word for the 'flesh shelves' on which the butchers who worked here for centuries displayed their meat. Today it's not the butchers who have taken charge but the wizards, as it is said to have been the inspiration for J. K. Rowling's Diagon Alley in the Harry Potter books.

As we walk between the houses down the narrow cobbled lane I can see the Harry Potter connection in every ancient handblown glass window pane. In fact, I spot at least three wizarding shopfronts among the sandwich bars, jewellers and clothing shops. You can get all sorts of artefacts here, including wands, broomsticks and gowns for the discerning witch or wizard. We press on to a microbrewery serving local ales, which we duly sample and follow with a couple more pints in the wonky-floored upstairs room of the Black Swan and then with a virtually recumbent meal in a bar with 1970s furniture and huge windows, giving us a chance to observe York's nocturnal population.

Despite the late time of year, we see teetering heels twisting on the cobbles. There is a lot more fake-tanned flesh on show than I'd expect: wobbling past our window come balloon-carrying hen-party gaggles in their finest skimperie. Rugger-buggers with Conan thighs threaten to tear apart stonewashed jeans as they waddle down the street half-drunk. In total contrast, we see the young Turks too, all skinny jeans and pointed suede shoes, mooning about in the darkened recesses of the partly lit streets: the cool kids rubbing shoulders – perhaps reluctantly – with the hoi polloi. The well-to-do are here as well, dressed up for a Saturday in the city: a little bit country, a little bit rock 'n' roll. Lip gloss and black party dresses, chinos and brogues walk brusquely past a guy looking for change. It's a bitter reminder that every wealthy city has its underclass, as he wanders from group to group, hoping for a little Saturday-night cheer to come his way.

I am enthralled. People watching on campsites doesn't have much variety to it, especially once you've exhausted the supply of fleeces and zip-off walking trousers, so I enjoy being able to observe all of humanity here. Tomorrow we shall be off to Rievaulx Abbey and Ryedale for more open-country exploring, but for now we are drinking in the slow road in the city.

It's an absolutely delightful shambles and we love it.

Helmsley
Traditional
Sweet
Shop

RYEDALE
H.D

HELMSLEY YORK
4      19
MILES  MILES

# THE DRIVING

York is small, with an inner ring road that encircles the old city walls. Everything inside, in my limited experience, is a nightmare, especially in a big motorhome. So be wary. That said, it's relatively easy to find your way on the Wigginton Road (B1363) past York Hospital out to where it is simply the B1363, towards Oswaldkirk and Helmsley.

The B1363 is largely flat as you leave York through farmland. It runs straight until you take a right-hand dogleg at Sutton-on-the-Forest. Thereafter, it weaves and wends its way through Brandsby, where the road begins to rise out of the levels into the Howardian Hills, Gilling East and Oswaldkirk, where it joins the B1257 and rolls on to Sproxton, where it meets the A170. At Oswaldkirk a slight hairpin bend takes you up the escarpment that marks a dramatic change between the Vale of York and the beginnings of the North York Moors National Park. To the west lies the awesome Sutton Bank, a steep 1-in-4 hill with a hairpin bend from which caravans are banned. It's worth a detour if you fancy a chug or a hair-raising descent, but be wary, it's a biggun!

From Sproxton the A170 takes you into Helmsley, one of my favourite
stops on this route. It's a truly delightful market town that's doing OK, thank
you, with arts centre, market, amazing deli, book shops and lots of local
buzz. The castle is lovely too, especially when viewed from over the wall.
The houses are a rich creamy yellow – York stone – and it feels like the
centre of the earth.

Heading north on the B1257, it's well worth a diversion to Rievaulx Abbey
down a steep hill into Ryedale. This is simply stunning – a creamy stone
village and the ruins of a once-powerful Cistercian monastery that was built
in 1132. Back on the B1257, you're up on the moors now, skirting between
pinnacles of open moorland along the banks of the River Seph, through
Chop Gate and Fangdale Beck, a wide-open dale with high ground to the
west and east.

Finally the road leads you to Clay Bank, the northern extremity of this part of the North York Moors. You must stop here and take in the views from the car park. They are just amazing, with views towards Middlesbrough and Stockton-on-Tees over the Cleveland plain. The descent is a little sad after such exhilarating, joyful driving, and it feels a bit less interesting, but still good, until you roll into Stokesley and pick up the A172 on your way towards Teesside. This is where it all changes and the hills begin to give way to urbanisation. But you're heading north, and that is a very fine thing.

## PLACES TO STAY

**York Rowntree Park Caravan Club Site**
Terry Avenue, York, North Yorkshire, YO23 1JQ
**web:** www.caravanclub.co.uk
**tel:** 01904 658997

**info:** *One of the club's most popular sites. Open all year, although if there's a lot of rain, watch out. The reception isn't built on stilts for nothing. Great location.*

**Helmsley Motorhome Parking**
Cleveland Way, Helmsley, YO62 5AT

**info:** *Overflow at Cleveland Way Car Park. Free overnight parking for motorhomes between 6.30 p.m. and 9.00 a.m. Great initiative started by the Board of Trade. Forward thinking! Don't abuse it.*

# IN THE AREA

**Rievaulx Abbey**  The ruins of a 12th-century abbey in a beautiful valley. Parking and café on site. Owned by English Heritage.
• www.english-heritage.org.uk/visit/places/rievaulx-abbey

**Helmsley Castle**  An impressive 900-year-old castle keep and remains of the old walls. Adjacent to motorhome parking and town centre.
• www.english-heritage.org.uk/visit/places/helmsley-castle

**York Minster**  One of England's loveliest cathedrals. It's been wowing Christians for over a thousand years with its creamy hues and total commitment to the Jesus thing.  • **yorkminster.org**

### Nearest van hire

**Taste of Freedom Motorhome Hire**
• www.tasteoffreedommotorhomes.co.uk

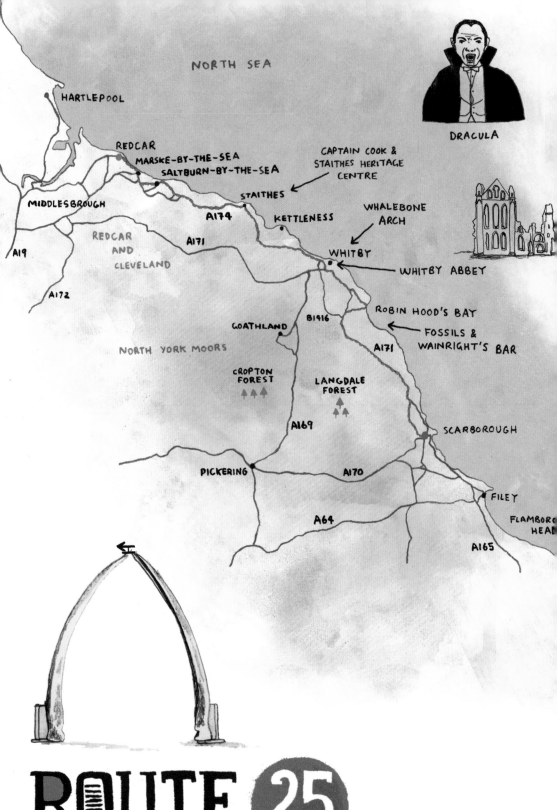

NORTH SEA

HARTLEPOOL

REDCAR
MARSKE-BY-THE-SEA
SALTBURN-BY-THE-SEA

MIDDLESBROUGH

A174

STAITHES

KETTLENESS

CAPTAIN COOK &
STAITHES HERITAGE
CENTRE

WHALEBONE
ARCH

WHITBY

WHITBY ABBEY

DRACULA

REDCAR
AND
CLEVELAND

A171

A19

A172

NORTH YORK MOORS

GOATHLAND

B1416

ROBIN HOOD'S BAY

FOSSILS &
WAINRIGHT'S BAR

A171

CROPTON
FOREST

LANGDALE
FOREST

A169

PICKERING

A170

SCARBOROUGH

A64

FILEY

FLAMBORO
HEAD

A165

ROUTE 25

# SALTBURN TO SCARBOROUGH

## FINDING SHELTER

The coast from Saltburn to Scarborough is an absolute joy. Why wouldn't it be? With brightly painted beach huts, long, elegant piers and traditional holiday fun times sitting side by side with tiny fishing villages and ports, there is a little of everything. If you take one coastal jaunt this year, make it here.

BEST FOR:
**Fishing villages**

START: **Redcar**

END:
**Scarborough**

MILEAGE: **45 miles (72 kilometres)**

DAYS TO EXPLORE: **2**

OS LANDRANGER MAP: **94, 101**

**Things have a habit of working out.** Wherever you are, wherever you go, someone will always be there to help you out. At least that's the way it has seemed to me while I have been writing this book. As the light fades and things begin to get fractious because there's no food or place to stay, something always happens to make the day.

It isn't looking that way, though, as I drop down the hill into Robin Hood's Bay. We've been scouring the local area for campsites and so far nothing has come good for us. The site I stayed at in Fylingdales on a previous visit looks deserted and unloved, while others appear to be in the same sad state of midwinter neglect. Even Britstops, the source of many a last-minute overnight save, has nothing to offer in the local area. I guess it's because of the geography in these parts: very few pubs have big enough car parks to accommodate a motorhome. Actually, scratch that: very few have car parks at all. The Bay Hotel, at the very bottom of the hill at Robin Hood's Bay, doesn't have a car park. Mind you, there isn't a lot of space for parking in Robin Hood's Bay at all. It's a tiny place, with one road in and out, a very steep hill and nowhere to leave a car, never mind a seven-metre-long motorhome.

It's almost as if the hill is dragging us in as we make our way to the village centre. There's

nowhere else to go except back the way we came – up the hill we've just driven down. We drive into the tiny car park at the bottom of the steep slope and almost get stuck. I do a few forwards and reverses, making up a seven-point turn. It's tight. It's getting tense in the motorhome. I stop and reach for the map. It seems as if there's nothing here for us tonight.

I hardly notice the man in the high-visibility jacket as I peer in the half-light at the map in front of me. But in a moment he is standing at my window, knocking gently on it with the knuckle of his forefinger. He wears a bobble hat and round glasses, has long white hair and a grey and white beard. He looks a bit like a wizard. He stands waiting for me to wind down the window.

'Hello.'

'Hello.'

'Are you looking for somewhere to stay?'

'Yes. There's nothing open.'

'I know. Try the car park at the old station. It's level and free.'

'Really? Wow. Does anyone mind?'

'No one minds. It's out of season.'

'Thank you.'

And with that he waves us off with a gesture that says 'don't mention it' before sauntering off.

We drive a little up the road, take a left and, after some manoeuvring, settle into a space like a dog seeking comfort on his favourite bean bag. It can sometimes take a while to get absolutely level. We consult the mini spirit level I keep in my 'box of useful things' and agree: it's almost bang on. We set the heating, pull back the bedclothes, pull on our coats and boots and hit the cool night air, looking for food and a drink.

We shuffle into the Bay Hotel at the bottom of the hill and find a place by the fire.

## THE DRIVING

The road from Saltburn to Scarborough has many moods. If you begin up the coast a little at Redcar Sands you'll feel the heat of the industrial North on the back of your neck as you look out to sea where the wind turbines turn gently offshore. Redcar's steelworks sit almost on the sand, facing off against the offshore wind like a battle between the old and the new, trapping beach walkers between the two. Even so, the beach is big and spacious.

The A1085 is the road that'll whisk you away from Redcar, joining up with the A174 just before Saltburn. This will take you all the way down to Whitby, where you'll need to join the A171 for the pootle down to Scarborough.

But don't get ahead of yourself. While the A174 doesn't follow the

coast like a coast road should, it's still going to take you to some pretty amazing places. Skinningrove is a post-industrial village that was taken over by ironworks in the 19th century. You can still see the slag-topped cliffs above the beach where small skiffs sit out the non-fishing days.

Further along the coast, at Staithes, it's a different picture. Staithes is celebrated because of its connection with Captain James Cook, who worked here for a time. It's a beautiful place, with art galleries, cafés and a pub, plus a lovely beach and quaint cobbled streets and steep alleyways.

Runswick Bay is another great stop, with its terracotta-tiled houses sitting in a steep valley and a huge beach stretching off to the south. Thereafter, things change a little as you drop down the steep hill to Sandsend and into Whitby. Sandsend is a brilliant spot for

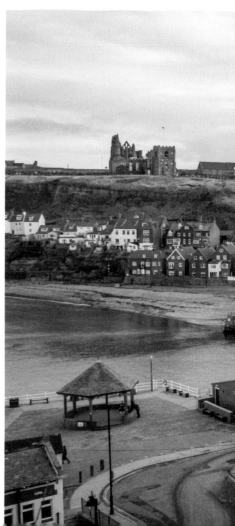

surfing, and the reef at the north end has some lovely fossils lined with fool's gold. Whitby, of course, is a Gothic joy, with chips and vampires in equal measure. I love it. Out of Whitby you'll get a real taste of the North York Moors as the main road – the A171 – heads inland. Diversions to Robin Hood's Bay and Ravenscar offer more fossil-hunting opportunities before you cross the moor and then drop down into lovely Victorian Scarborough. At Burniston take a left on to the A165 and enjoy the cruise into the town along the coastal road. This will bring you to Royal Albert Drive and then Marine Parade on North Bay. This is a cracking place to grab a spot and put the kettle on before continuing round the headland towards the marina and South Bay and all the trappings of seaside life that go with it.

## Nearest van hire

**North Yorkshire Motorhome Hire**
• www.northyorkshiremotor
homehire.com

## PLACES TO STAY

**Hooks House Farm Campsite**
Robin Hood's Bay, Whitby, North Yorkshire, YO22 4PE
**web:** www.hookshousefarm.co.uk
**tel:** 01947 880283

**info:** *Small vans and motorhomes only at this well-placed site in Robin Hood's Bay.*

**Cayton Village Caravan and Motorhome Club Site**
Mill Lane, Cayton Bay, Scarborough,
North Yorkshire, YO11 3NN
**tel:** 01723 583171

**info:** *All the usual facilities and luxuries for motorhomers, close to Scarborough and the wonderful Cayton Bay.*

# IN THE AREA

**The Cinder Track** An off-road walking and cycle route between Scarborough and Whitby along the bed of an old railway track.
▪ www.sustrans.org.uk/ncn/map/route/scarborough-to-whitby

**Sea Life** The undersea world in a tank at the north end of North Bay.
▪ www.visitsealife.com/scarborough

**Whitby Abbey** The Gothic, inspiring ruins of Whitby Abbey have led to all kinds of stories and horror fantasy. Unsurprising, considering it's a thousand-year-old ruin. ▪ www.english-heritage.org.uk/visit/places/whitby-abbey

**Wainwright's Bar** Situated at the end of the Coast to Coast Walk, as walked by Alfred Wainwright, on the slipway at Robin Hood's Bay. An old pair of boots and lots of cosy comforts. ▪ www.bayhotel.info

**Fossil Hunting** Yorkshire's Jurassic Coast is made of the same stuff as its slightly more popular cousin down south. There is plenty to find here, either in the rocks or embedded in the flat reefs. Lovely way to take a beach walk. ▪ www.ukfossils.co.uk/category/yorkshire

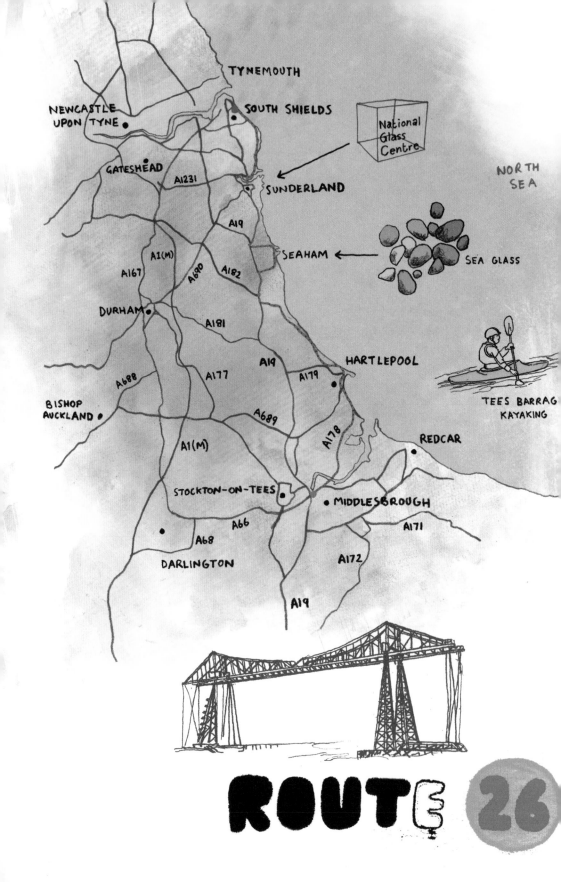

TYNEMOUTH

NEWCASTLE
UPON TYNE

SOUTH SHIELDS

National Glass Centre

NORTH SEA

GATESHEAD

A1231

SUNDERLAND

A19

SEAHAM

SEA GLASS

A1(M)

A167

A690

A182

DURHAM

A181

A19

HARTLEPOOL

A688

A177

A179

TEES BARRAG KAYAKING

BISHOP AUCKLAND

A689

A178

REDCAR

A1(M)

STOCKTON-ON-TEES

MIDDLESBROUGH

A66

A171

A68

A172

DARLINGTON

A19

ROUTE 26

# FROM TEESSIDE TO TYNESIDE

## THE GLASS ROUTE

Follow the coast north from Middlesbrough and you'll pass through some of England's most industrialised areas. But look carefully and you'll see beauty in abundance between the chimney stacks and cooling towers. You'll find beautiful beaches, nature reserves, glinting glass and a lot of very cool bridges.

BEST FOR: **Sea glass, bridges, glimmers of nature**

START: **Middles-brough**

END: **South Shields**

MILEAGE: **42 miles (68 kilometres)**

DAYS TO EXPLORE: **2**

OS LANDRANGER MAP: **88, 93**

We rise early to make the most of the light, or what little there is of it. There is a frost on the grass and a strong easterly breeze bringing cold sharp air from the North Sea. We pack up the motorhome, coiling stiff cables and hoses, putting away cold chocks and defrosting the windscreen. In the bluish light we see car lights on the A66 a few hundred metres away. It's commuting time.

We leave the site with a friendly wave from the wardens and pull into the traffic, heading towards Redcar and the Tees Transporter Bridge. Against the grey sky it looks like a badly drawn robot dog from a Star Wars movie, and I almost expect it to shake off its cables and make a dash for it. But it's not Hollywood around here.

We pull off the A66 and pass through an industrial estate, past Middlesbrough station and along deserted, forgotten streets. It's half industrial estate, half new-build housing here, with new developments sitting side by side with empty and rundown corrugated warehouses. The biggest structure for miles is the Transporter Bridge, blue and bright with steelwork.

We park up in the waiting area and wait for the gondola to arrive from the other bank of the Tees. It's empty. It glides into place quietly and we prepare to drive on to the structure that hangs on cables below the superstructure of the bridge. We wonder if we are too heavy to travel this way, as the weight limit is three tons, but no one bats an eyelid as we

drive on and park up. We pay our £1.30 to travel, and wait.

I love bridges. Taking the Transporter Bridge across the Tees is a first for me, so I am happy to mark the start of this next slow-road adventure with a trip on it. By the end of the day we will have crossed more than a few more mighty bridges, across the Wear and the Tyne, but for now we must set a course north along the coast in search of gems hidden among all the industrialisation.

Our first port of call is the RSPB centre at Saltholme, a lovely building set in the vast saltmarshes of the Tees estuary. It's surrounded by reeds and mudflats, and beyond that vast petrochemical plants, cooling towers, the Transporter Bridge and derelict stranded oil platforms. It's an incongruity, but it's also an oasis. We find the place has been yarn bombed, and there are triangles of brightly coloured knitted bunting welcoming us across the walkway to the main entrance. From the viewing platform we find our

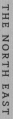

view of the marshes and cooling towers is brightened up by more knitting, as well as by scores of finches twittering in a tree. Between us and the towers there are hundreds of birds, out on the mudflats, flying overhead, wading in the shallows. It's as if nature is irrepressible, forcing a home for itself between the follies of man. I like it.

Later, at Seaham, we find jewels of sea glass on the beach, more moments of colour, and when we arrive as Sunderland's National Glass Centre we see its source. We watch as glassblowers create bottles before our eyes, in a vivid cobalt blue. It's mesmerising to see the bottle take shape and come to life, a reflection of the industry that once provided work for thousands in this area.

Did you know that all of the world's Pyrex was made in Sunderland? Me neither.

But I do now.

# THE DRIVING

The Caravan Club Site at the Tees Barrage is a great spot to explore the Durham coast. Just minutes from the Transporter Bridge, it is well connected and easy to find. Follow the A66 east past Middlesbrough station, following signs for the Transporter Bridge and the A178 to Hartlepool.

Once north of the Tees, follow the A178 past the monolithic chemical works and oil terminals towards Seaton Carew and Hartlepool Bay. At Hartlepool you can explore the narrow streets of the Headland, its red-brick houses and its marina, before taking the A1086 towards Peterlee, Easington Colliery and Seaham. You may have to take the A19 to Seaham from Easington, but it's only a short stretch and it makes the journey easier. Seaham Beach is a long stretch of sand and shingle that's unremarkable in many ways, apart from the fact that it's a treasure trove for sea-glass hunters. There used to be a huge bottle works at Seaham between the

1850s and 1921. Any glass that was spoiled was, apparently, dumped in the North Sea, where it would be tossed by the surf and made smooth and round by the wave action. Today it washes up on the beach there, making it a must-go destination for sea-glass hunters.

From Seaham, there's a great stretch of coast road (the B1287) on the way to the A1018. After that it's a rather uninteresting jaunt to Sunderland and the Wearmouth Bridge, another impressively industrial steel and rivet structure. Pick up the A183 to Roker for more coastal wanderings and the lovely lighthouse at Souter, as well as Marsden Rock at Marsden and the Grotto, a bar and restaurant built into the cliff face.

Finally, before you head inland up the Tyne to Gateshead to see the magnificent bridges of the Tyne, there is one last hurrah for this journey, and that's South Shields. The beach is fabulous and there are camping spots aplenty, although we stayed overnight in the car park adjacent to the Rattler, a friendly pub that's named after a railway that once carried colliery workers up and down the coast.

Nearest van hire

**Sweet Campers**
- www.sweetcampers.com

## PLACES TO STAY

**White Water Park Caravan and Motorhome Club Site**
Tees Barrage, Stockton-on-Tees, County Durham, TS18 2QW
**web:** www.caravanclub.co.uk
**tel:** 01642 634880

**info:** *Right on the Tees Barrage and therefore handy for watersports and the rest of the North East. Lovely wardens.*

# IN THE AREA

**RSPB Saltholme** An oasis among the reeds where you can sit and enjoy a cup of tea and a slice of cake while watching thousands of migrating birds and wildlife. Nice cake too.

• www.rspb.org.uk

**The Grotto** Below the cliff at Marsden is a grotto that's associated with some legendary stories. It was blasted out by a local sometime in the 18th century, became a place for smugglers and eventually became a bar. Nowadays you can take a lift down the cliff and enjoy great food in a unique spot overlooking Marsden Rock.

• www.marsdengrotto.com

**The Tees Barrage International White Water Centre**
An internationally famous white water rafting course, plus facilities and rental, where you can experience man-made white water just yards from your pitch. Looks impressive. Empty for the first time in years when I went.

• www.tbiwwc.com

**National Glass Centre** Here you can take a look at the glass trade's history and importance to Sunderland. Great exhibition centre (with a glass roof of course!) in the heart of Sunderland. Brilliant art, plus glass-making.

• www.nationalglasscentre.com

**Baltic Centre for Contemporary Art** Contemporary arts space on the south side of the Tyne at Gateshead. Nice café, brilliant gallery space. There is a lot more to Newcastle, but this is a lovely place in a great setting at the end of the route. Easy parking too!

• www.baltic.art

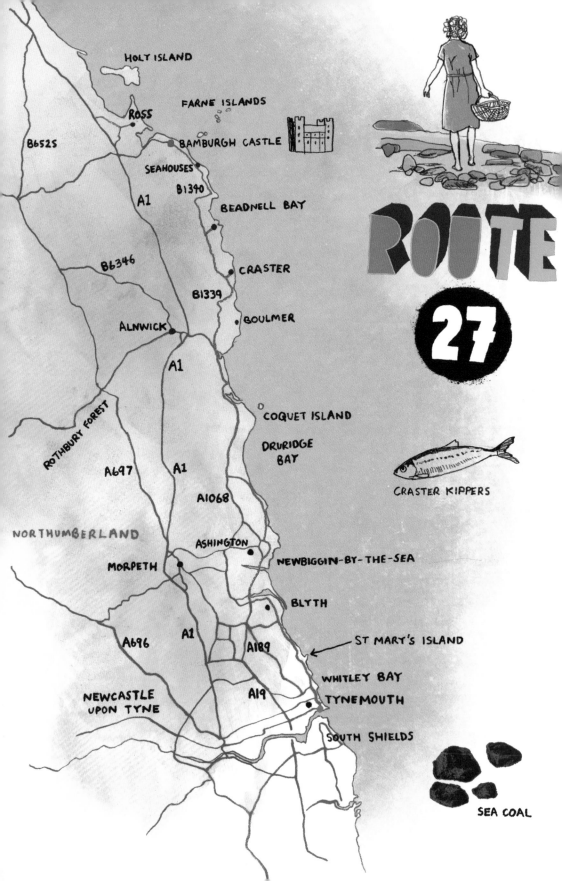

HOLT ISLAND

FARNE ISLANDS

ROSS

B652S

BAMBURGH CASTLE

SEAHOUSES

A1

B1340

BEADNELL BAY

B6346

CRASTER

B1339

ALNWICK

BOULMER

A1

COQUET ISLAND

ROTHBURY FOREST

DRURIDGE BAY

A697

A1

A1068

NORTHUMBERLAND

ASHINGTON

MORPETH

NEWBIGGIN-BY-THE-SEA

BLYTH

A696

A1

A189

ST MARY'S ISLAND

NEWCASTLE UPON TYNE

A19

WHITLEY BAY

TYNEMOUTH

SOUTH SHIELDS

ROUTE

27

CRASTER KIPPERS

SEA COAL

# TYNEMOUTH TO BAMBURGH

## WINTER IN PARADISE

The Northumberland coast, from Tynemouth in the south to Bamburgh in the north, is a treasure trove of riches. It has beautiful harbours, stunning castles, lovely beaches and fabulous driving. And the best thing of all is that it's quiet. Very, very quiet.

**BEST FOR:**
**Beaches and castles**

**START:**
**Tynemouth**

**END:**
**Bamburgh**

**MILEAGE:** 60 **miles (96 kilometres)**

**DAYS TO EXPLORE:** 3

**OS LANDRANGER MAP:** 93, 81, 75

As we pull out of Tynemouth, passing the castle and priory, it's snowing. Dark clouds, laden with snow, threaten from the north, blowing offshore from west to east out over the North Sea. It seems as if we are going to be chasing the sun, hoping for glimpses of sharp, thin winter sunshine between the storms that have been threatening for days. But we can't sit it out. We have to keep moving ever northwards to the zenith of this trip. We are heading for Bamburgh.

By the time we get to St Mary's Island at the far end of Whitley Bay the sky is clear except for a few vapour trails. The sun floods the windscreen with brightness and we stop to enjoy a stroll over that causeway before the tide floods it for another day. The lighthouse, tall and strong, dazzles against the blue sky.

That night we make it as far as Amble and settle for the night in a Britstop just outside the town. It's cold and clear so we walk into town to investigate a few pubs. The town has a lovely feel, even though it's quiet.

We rise early before it's light and layer up for a walk to the harbour. There has been a light dusting of snow, which is enough to give the town

a soft glow in the predawn. We make the first tracks down the icy streets. In the late 1980s Liz swam here with the peripatetic visitor Freddie the dolphin, so she's on a mission to work out where it was she slipped into the dark water and awaited his arrival. She can't quite get her bearings because there has been a lot of development since. There are huge 'sail loft'–type apartment blocks on the quaysides which sit side by side with the short, standard-issue Victorian terraced red-brick houses clustered around the bay. We walk along the pier and she tries to remember where she swam. It's so cold and dark that it seems improbable that anyone would ever want to swim in the brown water, but she assured me she did, a few times.

As the light improves the sun slowly makes its way up over the eastern horizon, gradually lighting up a row of cheerful beach huts at the head of the beach. I wait for a few minutes for the sun to light them up, my hands on the shutter in readiness, but it's too cold to linger. I stick my hands in my pockets and look around. The beach huts are jolly, which seems in contrast to the fishing boats and the gear that's piled up high on the quayside, in the same way that the new apartments seem out of place among the red-brick houses or the encrusted piles of the old pier. It is a place in the middle of great change, I think. At one time it must have been hard-working and tough. Now it's having a makeover, changing tack and becoming gentrified and popular, a Southwold of the North. I like it.

We wander over to Amble Beach and begin picking up litter, as we do wherever we go. There are lots of aluminium drink cans among the seaweed. We pick up for a few minutes before we see another figure hunched over a rock pool. He's carrying a red bucket and a coal shovel. I stop and chat with him about what he's up to and it turns out that he's looking for sea coal to put on the fire. We fall into conversation and he

tells us how he's been doing it for over 50 years. He's the last one who still bothers – even though he has central heating – because the sea coal is getting scarce. But, as he says, the point is about getting out, making an effort and refusing to buckle under to the cold weather or the winter.

He looks as though he's in his seventies, but he tells us he's 80 years young. We can believe him.

A few more miles to the north is Bamburgh, Northumberland's crowning glory, the beautifully situated castle sitting atop a rocky promontory overlooking the North Sea. There is evidence that the site has been occupied for over 10,000 years. Over the centuries many have come and gone and left their mark, however small, on this landscape. Bamburgh has seen saints, Iron Age people, Saxons, Christians, Romans, Normans and wealthy Victorian philanthropists. Its final shape was determined by the great restoration work that was carried out on it, starting in 1894, and costing over a million pounds, which, I gather, was a lot of cash in those days.

We park in the car park below the castle only to find that in winter it's open only at the weekend. But no bother. We pull on our boots and walk through

the dunes to the beach, eager to seek out the view of the castle we all know. The wind is blowing hard and it's cold but sunny (such a refreshing change from the weather at home in Cornwall in January, which tends to be wet and miserable) and the top layer of sand is blowing across the beach in wispy waves around our ankles. The light is perfect, warm and deep, casting long shadows due to the time of day and year. I am in raptures and clicking away. The castle, reflected in the thin film of water left by the receding waves, looks perfect.

It is perfect.

# THE DRIVING

I wish I could say that the drive from Tynemouth to Bamburgh was straightforward and easy, a jaunt along the coast on a continuous strip of smooth tarmac – but it isn't. However, once you hit the road you'll realise that it's a coastline with many possibilities. You can drive it in a few hours if you want to race along or you can stop at regular intervals to enjoy the beach – or the beaches – or the castles. From Tynemouth follow Rockcliff Gardens, then the Promenade along the coast to the A193. You need to follow this road through Blyth and hit the A189 for Amble and Newbiggin-by-the-Sea. This is the only bit of dual carriageway I want you to drive along today, so enjoy it … then turn off as quickly as you can and head for Lynemouth and Cresswell for a dune-backed drive with lots of stop-offs, then take another detour when you get to Druridge Bay, and another at Alnmouth. You won't believe you'll be able to find a better beach, until you turn the next corner. At Embleton Bay you'll think you died and went to heaven, if beach huts are what take your fancy. There are some wonderfully ramshackle examples above the beach here.

Past Amble and Alnmouth follow the B1339 towards Bamburgh, and then follow your nose towards the coast to find Craster, Embleton, Benthall, Beadnell and finally Bamburgh on the B1340. Each offshoot will bring you to somewhere new and different. Seahouses has a curious set of seats overlooking the harbour, like a terrace watching some football game. Few people were perching there in January, but in summer it must get quite busy, I imagine.

## PLACES TO STAY

### The Camping and Caravan Club Site at Bellingham

Brown Rigg, Bellingham, Hexham, Northumberland, NE48 2JY

**web:** www.campingandcaravanningclub.co.uk

**tel:** 01434 220175

**info:** *Open most of the year, offering a place to dry the boots, fill the tanks and recharge the motorhome.*

# IN THE AREA

**Bamburgh Castle**  This is the quintessential castle on the beach, even though it's has been remodelled a few times over the years. Some might say it's a Victorian folly, but it's still *very* impressive to walk on Bamburgh Beach and see the castle in the dunes.  • www.bamburghcastle.com

**Holy Island**  A little to the north of Bamburgh is the Holy Island of Lindisfarne, a tidal island with a priory and castle. It's visited by 650,000 people a year, some of whom get cut off by the tide! A lovely place for a day out.  • www.lindisfarne.org.uk

**Craster Kippers**  Craster is the home of the kipper, and many have been smoked here, although only one smokery remains these days. Go and fetch a couple for breakfast!  • www.kipper.co.uk

**Warkworth Castle**  Another fine ruin on the Northumberland coast. They chose its location well, just a mile inland from Amble. Lovely cream-coloured stone and great views … what else do you need?  • www.english-heritage.org.uk/visit/places/warkworth-castle-and-hermitage

Nearest van hire

**Castle Coast Campers Ltd**
 • www.castlecoastcampers.co.uk

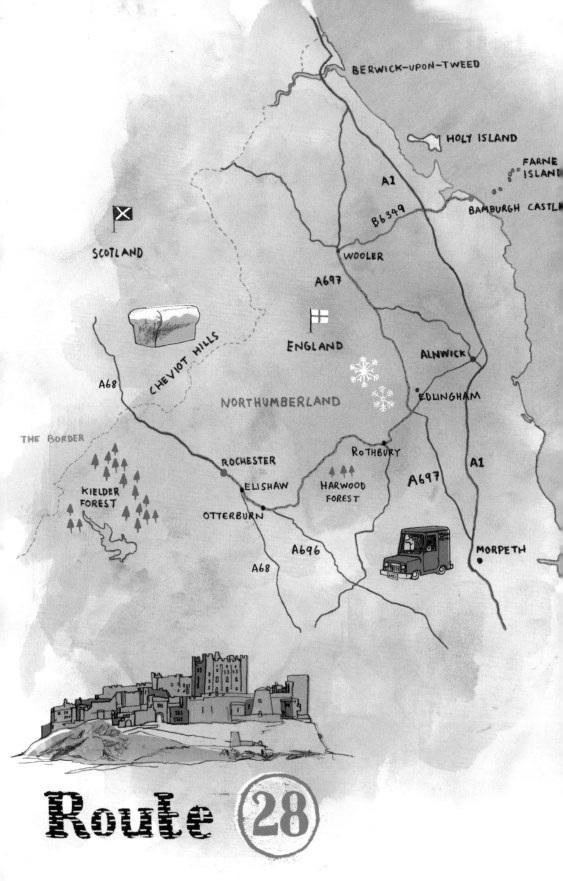

BERWICK-UPON-TWEED

HOLY ISLAND

FARNE ISLANDS

A1

B6349

BAMBURGH CASTLE

SCOTLAND

WOOLER

A697

CHEVIOT HILLS

ENGLAND

ALNWICK

A68

NORTHUMBERLAND

EDLINGHAM

THE BORDER

ROTHBURY

ROCHESTER

A697

A1

ELISHAW

HARWOOD FOREST

KIELDER FOREST

OTTERBURN

A696

MORPETH

A68

# Route ②⑧

# BAMBURGH TO ROCHESTER

## SNOWED IN!

There's more to Northumberland than just the coast. Inland it has Europe's largest man-made forest as well as vast tracts of moorland. I took the slow road across country from Bamburgh to Rochester to get closer to the National Park, but all I got was snowed in. Still, it was very pretty.

BEST FOR: **Big vistas and open country**

START: **Bamburgh**

END: **Rochester**

MILEAGE: **50 miles (80 kilometres)**

DAYS TO EXPLORE: **1**

OS LANDRANGER MAP: **75, 80, 81**

THE NORTH EAST

339

It is beautiful at Bamburgh. The sun is casting a golden light on the yellow sands of the beach and the castle is looking pretty much picture-perfect in the late-afternoon light. As it's January there's nowhere to stay locally so we decide to drive across country to Rochester where we know there is a Britstop and a campsite we can pitch up at. There are few roads traversing the National Park, so we plot a route that will take us around it and that will eventually lead us into it.

There is ice on the road so it's a tense drive. We cross the A1 and head up towards Wooler, where we hit the A697 and then take a detour towards Rothbury. Until now we've been travelling parallel to the Cheviot Hills, which rise like white-topped loaves to our right, but now we turn off towards them, into the park and the high ground, and all the unpredictability that brings.

We head into the park. The road is beautiful, taking us between the hills of Harwood Forest to the south and the National Park to our north and west, but not before we've crossed Rothbury Forest.

By the time we reach the A68 at Otterburn it's snowing heavily and I'm getting jittery. We need to stop soon or I fear we'll be looking for somewhere to spend the night at the side of the road. We locate our nearest Britstop, at the Redesdale Arms, and decide to make a dash for it. But it means heading further into the park, further up into the Cheviots and further into the storm. What other choice do we have? The nearest campsite, at the Boe Rigg, just outside Hexham, is a further ten miles or so and would mean taking the smaller roads. I will admit I quite fancy it, but I am overruled. The last time we were there a man pulled up in a pick-up truck wearing triple denim, a cowboy hat and spurs. I liked the vibe, but not tonight.

We turn right, into the blizzard, and make our way to the Redesdale Arms. We miss the turn-off and then face the prospect of having to make a U-turn in Cottonshop. It's icy and getting worse, but we manage to slip and slide our way up the steep drive and into the car park through deep drifts. We dash into the pub and check it's OK for us to stay. They direct us to a place to park and we pull in, doubtful that we'll be able to get out. We set up and realise the gas has run out.

It's a warm evening by the fire at the Redesdale Arms. The food is great and the atmosphere is friendly. When we retire to the van it's not so warm. The heating has been off for an hour or two and there is no gas to cook on. It's a double-duvet kind of a night.

We wake to a quiet, snowy Northumberland, dress quickly and head out into the car park. About four inches of snow has fallen overnight and it looks like we might not get out in a hurry. The sky is turning pink and purple as we wander up to the nature reserve that's at the back of the pub. We walk through the woods on a wooden walkway that leads us to an encampment next to a stream that looks like it's used for a forest school. It's a beautiful morning to be alive. We survived a night in the van and now all we have to do is eat and then dig ourselves out.

It doesn't take long. Thank goodness the landlady turned up with a bag of rock salt.

# THE DRIVING

This is a lovely slow road to take if you don't want to schlepp back to Newcastle to get into the National Park from Bamburgh. It has moments of revelation and delight as you travel through forests, farmland and open country, always looking to the hills to the north.

From Bamburgh take the B6349 towards Wooler, where you'll join the A697, one of the main routes between Scotland and England on the east coast. It's a long, straight-ish road that can be heavy with haulage traffic. Once you reach Edlingham take a right on the B6341 towards Rothbury and you'll start to feel like you're in the wilds. In parts like a drive through Buckinghamshire, part Dales and part wild country, it's an interesting, winding drive through 'Postman Pat' land. You'll follow the River Coquet for a while before turning away from the river and heading to Otterburn.

At the A696 turn right towards Scotland before joining the A68 at Elishaw.

From here you can carry on to Scotland over the Cheviots or, in the summer, take a left down the forest drive that links up with Kielder on the other side of Emblehope Moor. It was closed when I visited in winter because of rockfalls and potholes, but if you fancy a challenge, go for it. Just make sure you pack away the Wedgwood before you do.

## PLACES TO STAY

**The Redesdale Arms**
Rochester, Nr Otterburn,
Northumberland, NE19 1TA
**web:** www.redesdale-arms.co.uk
**email:** info@ redesdale-arms.co.uk
**tel:** 01830 520668

**info:** *A great Britstop stopping-off point between Scotland and England on the A68. As such, it's also known locally as the First and Last.*

**The Boe Rigg Campsite**
Charlton, Northumberland,
NE48 1PE
**web:** www.theboerigg.co.uk
**email:** hi@theboerigg.co.uk
**tel:** 01434 240663

**info:** *The Boe Rigg, just outside Hexham, is our kind of place. We didn't stay but would have loved to, and will next time we visit. There are rooms, plus camping, an excellent restaurant and bar and very friendly staff. Go and see them, say hello and wish that every campsite could be like this.*

# IN THE AREA

**Kielder Forest Cycle Routes**  Kielder Water & Forest Park is a
fantastic place for off-road cycling. There are easy routes for all the
family that circumnavigate the reservoir – giving wonderful views over the
water – as well as some serious off-road stuff for more daring singletrack
adventures. The blue-grade 'Osprey Trail' is one of the toughest, but most
rewarding, routes of its type I have ridden.  • **www.thebikeplace.co.uk**

**Starry Skies at Kielder**  Northumberland is home to an International
Dark Sky Park, with the largest area of protected night sky in Europe.
That means it's one of the best places to go stargazing in England.
The vast and empty landscape
has little light pollution, so on
clear nights you can marvel
at celestial beauty of all kinds.
• **www.kielderobservatory.org**

Nearest van hire

**Castle Coast Campers Ltd**
• www.castlecoastcampers.co.uk

# CAMPER VAN AND MOTORHOME HIRE

**CAMPERVANTASTIC LTD**
Unit 5, 118 Stanstead Road,
Forest Hill, London, SE23 1BX
**Website:** www.campervan
tastic.com
**Email:** hire@campervan
tastic.com
**Telephone:** 020 8291 6800
**Info:** 20 mixed vans,
including VW California
Ocean camper van, VW
California Beach camper
van, Mercedes Benz Marco
Polo camper van, VW Grand
California 600 motorhome

**CASTLE COAST
CAMPERS LTD**
4 Mill View, Hart,
Nr Hartlepool, County
Durham, TS27 3AL
**Website:** www.castlecoast
campers.co.uk
**Email:** hello@castlecoast
campers.co.uk
**Telephone:** 07939 955165
**Info:** 2 x 1972 VW Westfalia
Campmobile (1 Crossover,
1 Twin Slider), 1 x 1973
VW Westfalia Continental

**COAST2COAST
CAMPER HIRE**
Heathfield Farm, Oil Mill
Lane, Exeter, Devon, EX5 1AN
**Website:** coast2coast
camperhire.co.uk
**Email:** info@coast2coast
camperhire.co.uk
**Telephone:** 07952 571966
**Info:** 4 x 1971 VW Type 2
camper vans

**COLUMBUS CAMPERVANS**
Grovesend, Swansea, SA4 4WE
**Website:** www.columbus
campervans.com
**Email:** hello@columbus
campervans.com
**Telephone:** 07504 980321
**Info:** 2 x 1973 VW Type 2
Westfalia, 1 x VW Type 2 Viking

**KERNOW KAMPERS**
41 Ventonlace, Grampound,
Cornwall, TR2 4TA
**Website:** www.kernow-
kampers.com
**Email:** admin@kernow-
kampers.com
**Telephone:** 01726 884689
**Info:** 2-, 4- and 6-berth luxury
Adria motorhomes; minidub
camper vans and Japanese
import mini-campers

**LAKES CAMPER HIRE**
10–12 Woolpack Yard,
Kendal, Cumbria, LA9 4NG
**Website:** www.lakescamper
hire.co.uk
**Email:** info@lakescamper
hire.co.uk
**Telephone:** 07973 691595
**Info:** 2 x T5 VW camper vans

**MOOVANS
CAMPERVAN RENTALS**
Minstrell Farm, Withy Road,
Highbridge, Somerset,
TA9 3NW
**Website:** www.moovans.com
**Email:** info@moovans.com
**Telephone:** 07702 542646
**Info:** 3 x new T5 and T6
luxury VW camper vans

**NORTH YORKSHIRE
MOTORHOME HIRE**
Deerholme Farm, High
Marishes, Yorkshire,
YO17 6UQ
**Website:** www.northyorkshire
motorhomehire.com
**Email:** northyorkshire motor
homehire@gmail.com
**Telephone:** 07393 354208
**Info:** 1 x Carioca 706,
1 x VW T5 camper van